THE EDITORS

Ken Pickering is the author of many books on the, practice, study and teaching of theatre and has combined the careers of playwright, director, actor and academic. He was Professor of Theatre at Gonzaga University in Washington State and is now Honorary Professor in the Drama Department at the University of Kent. He was co-founder of the Institute for the Arts in Therapy and Education in London.

Anthea Preston is a professional actress and drama teacher with wide experience of running a theatre company with her husband, Harry, and in presenting performances for children in schools. She has devised and performed in many of her own plays and has appeared in numerous theatre productions as well as TV and Film. Her family have all been involved in aspects of dance and theatre.

Although this is their first collaboration in publishing, Ken and Anthea have combined on a substantial number of highly successful theatre projects including the touring plays *Vita and Harold, The Immortal Harvey* and *Monday Nights have Got to be Better* together with *The Midlands Mysteries* in Birmingham Cathedral.

ACKNOWLEDGEMENTS

The Editors gratefully acknowledge the permission to use copyright material as follows:
Macmillan Children's books for *William in Trouble*, Oxford University Press for *A London Child of the 1870s*, Faber and Faber for *Period Piece* and *The Life and Works of Harold Pinter*, Serpent's Tale Publishing for *A Forties Child*, Jonathan Cape for *The Life of Graham Greene Vol. 1*, Macmillan for *Joyce Grenfell Requests the Pleasure*, Palgrave Macmillan for *Theatre and Education* and The History Press for *Richmal Crompton; the woman behind Just William*.

The Editors wish to express their gratitude to their families and friends who have contributed to and allowed themselves to be part of this book; to Professor Helen Nicholson for her encouragement; to Ildiko Solti and Irene Pickering for their tireless work on the typescript and to our publisher, David, for giving us this opportunity.

Cover illustration by Denys Le Fevre, courtesy of David Rankin

ISBN: 978-1-84944-157-5

British Library Cataloguing in Publication Data.
A catalogue record for this book is available from the British Library.

Published by UKUnpublished.

UKUnpublished
.CO.UK

www.ukunpublished.co.uk
info@ukunpublished.co.uk

THEATRE: THE FIRST STAGES

A collection of early experiences

EDITED AND INTRODUCED

BY

KEN PICKERING

WITH

ANTHEA PRESTON

FOREWORD BY DR MARGOT SUNDERLAND

CONTENTS

FOREWORD BY Dr MARGOT SUNDERLAND
(Founder Director of the Institute for the Arts in Therapy and Education and the Centre for Child Mental Health, London.)

This excellent book written by two of the most eminent exponents and authors in the field of theatre and drama education is a 'must' for any parent or child professional who truly cares about fostering their child's imagination and creativity to the full. The moving and deeply touching accounts of early encounters with theatre, show just how powerful and life changing these can be, whether in the form of actual theatre or, as the book explores, those 'spontaneous theatricals' that happen in the home from time to time: that is, if parents and families provide the culture vital to support such delightful happenings.

The book brings home the fact that theatre is one of the most profound embodiments of the human imagination, and so early encounters with theatre's alternative often utterly absorbing worlds is not simply another play event in the child's life but often deeply memorable and actually life changing The book bears this out in that many of the writers whose memories are recorded show how these early encounters enriched and had a major long- term beneficial effect at both a personal and professional level.

Overall this book fills a vital gap in the available literature on child psychology and educational drama and is essential reading for anyone intent on enabling children to thrive and use life well.

THEATRE: THE FIRST STAGES

A collection of early experiences

'In my theatre at least, life was as I chose to make it'
(C. Henry Warren: *A Boy in Kent* 1937)

Can you imagine a world without imagination? A world entirely composed of what we like to call 'reality'. A world without stories , music, dancing, fantasy, pottery, painting, poetry, plays, games, fashion, design, film, musicals, jokes, comedy, memories, dreams, ambitions? Without imagination we live in total emotional poverty; the employment of the imagination and its nourishment are essential and fundamental human activities.

Children explore the process of living through their imaginations: this is why they create strange names for their imaginary friends; why playwrights like Harold Pinter peopled their childhood world with imaginary characters and Richmal Crompton, the creator of the 'Just William' books made up plays to act at home without any need for 'drama lessons'. It is why children respond to fantasy and to stories about wolves and tigers and wizards and why child psychotherapists increasingly attempt to unlock the feelings of traumatised children through fantasy, metaphor and the arts.

Theatre is one of the supreme embodiments of the imagination of childhood. It takes its participants and audiences into alternative worlds and can be shaped and controlled in way that 'real' life can never be. We can watch and listen to children as they invent dialogue between their toys or assemble a drama on an imaginary battlefield. We can join in their fantasies by hiding in a bush or turn their bedrooms into the cockpit of an aeroplane. Sadly, we can also see children who are starved of the opportunity of imaginative play, who are forced to adopt adult values and performance ideas too soon and who never create stories or dances or music or pictures as natural aspects of their lives: and we witness their drab, empty and emotionally crippled existence.

Many of the writers whose memories are recorded in this book went on to distinguished careers in aspects of drama but some built on those early experiences to enrich other professional and personal achievements, simply benefiting from the educational power of theatre. That power can be experienced at a very young age: indeed, we often overlook how live performance can absorb those in the early years of childhood. When Images Theatre Company was touring its programmes of live poetry performances for presentation to children in public libraries there was often an expectation from library co-ordinators that children of 'reception age' would not be participating. Dialogues with the directors of the company often went as follows:

'We would not expect the reception class to participate'

'No, please let them join in'

'But they're only 4'

'That's fine, we're used to 4yr olds'

'Well, we can take them out if they get restless'

'Well that's never happened so far'

And it never did.

When the same company was presenting the play *Vita and Harold* at the Theatre Royal in Margate, the son of the leading actress said that he was going to bring his six-year-old daughter to see the performance. He was reminded that the play was very 'wordy', being based on diaries and letters with fairly minimal action. However, the young girl remained totally absorbed and focussed throughout the two hour performance and, in fact, brought more to the role of being an audience that many adults. Here was a child reared on stories and imagination for whom even an 'adult' play was merely an extension of earlier experience.

There are, of course, many stories of children from theatrical families who virtually grew up in dressing rooms and rehearsals and went into the theatre in later life as if it were the most obvious thing to do. However, even more fascinating are the accounts of the spontaneous 'theatricals' that were part of many homes and childhoods. Examples of these have been evoked in fiction but others are preserved for us in the true recollections included in this book. What, perhaps, strikes one most is the elaborate yet improvised nature of such activities. Some were clearly the result of childhood experiences of the live theatre but others were simply driven by imagination and creativity.

Pessimists might argue that all this is in the past and that television, computers and ever more sophisticated entertainment technology have stifled the passion for imagination and live performance; but there is plenty of evidence to the contrary. The huge success of the Stagecoach franchise of weekend theatre schools for young people and some of their imitators has demonstrated an almost indelible desire for theatrical activity.

Involving children in such activity is by no means new. As long ago as the eighteenth century, many young people gained their first experience of performing under the auspices of the remarkable Sarah Thorne, who was the licensee and manager of Margate's beautiful Theatre Royal (which we have already mentioned) and remains in use today as the second oldest theatre in Britain. At her premises on the opposite side of Hawley Square she offered classes in acting, make-up and voice production according the styles of the day and the students were gradually given opportunities to take part in the productions at the theatre, which they reached via a tunnel that had originally, it is thought, been built and used by smugglers!

Recent research has demonstrated just how much Marlowe, Shakespeare and their contemporaries relied on child performers from choirs and the Chapel Royal and it would seem that, even now, however hard we try to blunt the imagination or prevent children from dressing up or satisfy their need for performance and story-telling with so called 'reality' we fail. And the more we attempt to relegate drama and theatre to 'non-curriculum' subjects, in their education, the more popular they become. The ability of young people to utilise their imaginations was demonstrated recently by an actor who had just finished a period of working with the Royal Shakespeare Company. He adapted Shakespeare's play *Macbeth* as a 'two-handed' performance for secondary schools, focussing on the relationship between Macbeth and Lady Macbeth with the other events of the play only mentioned. Accompanied by stunning sound-effects and a specially commissioned score the play was presented without scenery or 'props'. Recalling the production, its creator said that, in discussion with the audiences, who watched in absolute silence, there was agreement that 'they could see the blood on our hands'.

So, as you dip into and enjoy this book 'On your imaginary forces work'

LOUISA M.ALCOTT

(1832-1888)

One of the most memorable and vivid evocations of a childhood permeated by home-made drama and theatre is contained in Louisa Alcott's semi-autobiographical novel, *Little Women.*(1868) This classic piece of young people's fiction is set in a New England home in the early years of the nineteenth century and tells the story of four girls: Margaret (Meg), Jo (based on the character of the writer), Amy and Elizabeth (Beth). The family experienced hard times because their father had left to fight in the civil war and the four girls were forced to create their own entertainment. In this, they were remarkably successful, largely because of Jo's passion for literature and acting. During the course of the novel the girls act out *The Pilgrim's Progress* and their own version of *The Pickwick Papers* but it is their Christmas plays that are described in such compelling and amusing detail.

The book opens with the approach of what promises to be a rather difficult Christmas but the sheer invention and imagination of the four young people creates a feast of theatre and enjoyment.

Our first extract provides an account of a lesson in melodramatic acting given by Jo to her more reluctant and retiring sisters and, no doubt, fuelled by her romantic reading. She combines the roles of playwright, actress and producer!
The extract is entitled 'Playing Pilgrims':

"I don't mean to act any more after this time; I'm getting too old for such things," observed Meg, who was as much a child as ever about "dressing up" frolics.

"You won't stop, I know, as long as you can trail round in a white gown with your hair down, and wear gold-paper jewellery. You are the best actress we've got, and there'll be an end of everything if you quit the boards," said Jo. "We ought to rehearse to-night; come here, Amy, and do the fainting scene, for you are as stiff as a poker in that."

"I can't help it; I never saw anyone faint, and I don't choose to make myself all black and blue, tumbling flat as you do. If I can go down easily I'll drop; if I can't, I shall fall into a chair and be graceful; I don't care if Hugo does come at me with a pistol," returned Amy, who was not gifted with dramatic power, but was chosen because she was small enough to be borne out shrieking, by the hero of the piece.

Do it this way; clasp your hand so, and stagger across the room, crying frantically, 'Roderigo, save me! save me!'" And away went Jo, with a melodramatic scream which was truly thrilling.

Amy followed but she poked her hands out stiffly before her, and jerked herself along as if she went by machinery; and her "Ow!" was more suggestive of pins being run into her than of fear and anguish. Jo gave a despairing groan, and Meg laughed outright, while Beth let her bread burn as she watched the fun with interest.

"It's no use! Do the best you can when the time comes, and if the audience shout, don't blame me. Come on, Meg."

Then things went smoothly, for Don Pedro defied the world in a speech of two pages without a single break; Hagar, the witch, chanted an awful incantation over her kettleful of simmering toads, with weird effect; Roderigo rent his chains asunder manfully, and Hugo died in agonies of remorse and arsenic, with a wild "Ha! Ha!"

"It's the best we've had yet," said Meg, as the dead villain sat up and rubbed his elbows.

"I don't see how you can write and act such splendid things, Jo. You're a regular Shakespeare!" exclaimed Beth, who firmly believed that her sisters were gifted with wonderful genius of all things.

"Not quite," replied Jo, modestly. I do think 'The Witch's Curse, an Operatic Tragedy,' is rather a nice thing; but I'd like to try *Macbeth*, if only to do the killing part. 'Is that a dagger that I see before me?'" muttered Jo, rolling her eyes, and clutching at the air, as she had seen a famous tragedian do.

Our second extract describes the Christmas performance itself. It is entitled 'A merry Christmas':

On Christmas night, a dozen girls piled onto the bed, which was the dress circle, and sat before the blue and yellow chintz curtains in a most flattering state of expectancy. There was a good deal of rustling and whispering behind the curtain, and presently the bell sounded, the curtains flew apart, and the 'Operatic Tragedy' began.

"A gloomy wood", according to the one play-bill, was represented by a few shrubs in pots, a green baize on the floor, and a cave in the distance. This cave was made with a clothes-horse for a roof, bureaux for walls; and in it was a small furnace in full blast, with a black pot on it, and an old witch bending over it. A moment was allowed for the first thrill to subside; then Hugo, the villain, stalked in with a clanking sword at his side, a slouched hat, black beard, mysterious cloak, and the boots. After pacing to and fro in much agitation, he struck his forehead, and burst out in a wild strain, singing of his hatred of Roderigo, his love for Zara, and his pleasing resolution to kill the one and win the other. The audience applauded the moment he paused for breath, and, bowing with the air of one accustomed to public praise, he ordered Hagar to come forth with a commanding "What ho! Minion! I need thee!"

Out came Meg, with grey horse-hair hanging about her face, a red and black robe, a staff, and cabalistic signs upon her cloak. Hugo demanded a potion to make Zara adore him, and one to destroy Roderigo. Hagar, in a fine dramatic melody, promised both, and proceeded to call up the spirit who would bring the love philtre:-

> "Hither, hither, from thy home,
>   Airy sprite, I bid thee come!
>   Born of roses, fed on dew,
>   Charms and potions canst thou brew?
>   Bring me here, with elfin speed,
>   The fragrant philtre which I need;
>   Make it sweet, and swift and strong;
>   Spirit, answer now my song!"

A soft strain of music sounded, and then at the back of the cave appeared a little figure in cloudy white, with glittering wings, golden hair, and a garland of roses in its head. Waving a wand, it sung:-

> "Hither I come

From my airy home,
Afar in the silver moon;
 Take the magic spell,
 Oh, use it well!
Or its power will vanish soon.

and dropping a small gilded bottle at the witch's feet, the spirit vanished. Another chant from Hagar produced another apparition – not a lovely one, for with a bang, an ugly, black imp appeared, and having croaked a reply, tossed a dark bottle at Hugo, and disappeared with a mocking laugh. Having warbled his thanks, and put the potions in his boots, Hugo departed; and Hagar informed the audience that, as he had killed a few of her friends in times past, she had cursed him, and intended to thwart his plans, and be revenged on him. Then the curtain fell, and the audience reposed and ate candy while discussing the merits of the play.

A good deal of hammering went on before the curtain rose again; but when it became evident what a masterpiece of stage-carpentering had been got up, no one murmured at the delay. It was truly superb! A tower rose to the ceiling; half-way up appeared a window with a lamp burning at it, and behind the white curtain appeared Zara in a lovely blue and silver dress, waiting for Roderigo. He came, in gorgeous array, with plumed cap, red cloak, chestnut love-locks, a guitar, and the boots, of course. Kneeling at the front of the tower, he sung a serenade in melting tones. Zara replied, and after a musical dialogue, consented to fly. Then came the grand effect of the play. Roderigo produced a rope-ladder with five steps to it, threw up one end, and invited Zara to descend. Timidly she crept from her lattice, put her hand on Roderigo's shoulder, and was about to leap gracefully down, when, "alas, alas for Zara!" she forgot her train – it caught in the window; the tower tottered, leaned forward, fell with a crash, and buried the unhappy lovers in the ruins!

A universal shriek arose as the russet boots waved wildly from the wreck, and a golden head emerged, exclaiming, "I told you so! I told you so!" With wonderful presence of mind Don Pedro, the cruel sire, rushed in, dragged out his daughter with a hasty aside –

"Don't laugh, act as if it was all right!" and ordering Roderigo up, banished him from the kingdom with wrath and scorn. Though decidedly shaken by the fall of the tower upon him, Roderigo defied the old gentleman, and refused to stir. This dauntless example fired Zara; she also defied her sire, and he ordered them both to the deepest dungeons of the castle. A stout little retainer came in with chains, and led them away, looking very much frightened, and evidently forgetting the speech he ought to have made.

Act three was the castle hall; and here Hagar appeared, having come to free the lovers and to finish Hugo. She hears him coming, and hides; sees him put the potions into two cups of wine, and bid the timid little servant "Bear them to the captives in their cells, and tell them I shall come anon." The servant takes Hugo aside to tell him something, and Hagar changes the cups for two others which are harmless. Ferdinando, the "minion", carries them away, and Hagar puts back the cup which holds the poison meant for Roderigo. Hugo, getting thirsty after a long warble, drinks it, loses his wits, and after a good deal of clutching and stamping, falls flat and dies.

This was a truly thrilling scene; though some persons might have thought that the sudden tumbling down of a quantity of long hair rather marred the effect of the villain's death.

Act four displayed the despairing Roderigo on the point of stabbing himself, because he has been told that Zara has deserted him. Just as the dagger is at his heart, a lovely song is sung under his window, informing him that Zara is true, but in danger, and he can save her if he will. A key is thrown in, which unlocks the door, and in a spasm of rapture he throws off his chains, and rushes away to find and rescue his lady-love.

Act five opened with a stormy scene between Zara and Don Pedro. He wishes her to go into a convent, but she won't hear of it; and after a touching appeal, is about to faint, when Roderigo dashes in and demands her hand. Don Pedro refuses because he is not rich. They shout and gesticulate tremendously, but cannot agree, and Roderigo is about to bear away the exhausted Zara, when the timid servant enters with a letter and a bag from Hagar, who has mysteriously disappeared. The letter informs the party that she bequeaths untold wealth to the young pair, and an awful doom to Don Pedro if he doesn't make them happy. The bag is opened, and several quarts of tin money shower down upon the stage, till it is quite glorified with the glitter. This entirely softens the "stern sire"; he consents without a murmur, all join in a joyful chorus, and the curtain falls upon the lovers kneeling to receive Don Pedro's blessing, in attitudes of the most romantic grace.

Tumultuous applause followed, but received an unexpected check; for the cot-bed on which the "dress circle" was built, suddenly shut up, and extinguished the enthusiastic audience. Roderigo and Don Pedro flew to the rescue, and all were taken out unhurt, though many were speechless with laughter. The excitement had hardly subsided when Hannah appeared, with "Mrs March's compliments, and would the ladies walk down to supper?"

This was a surprise, even to the actors; and when they saw the table they looked at one another in rapturous amazement. There was ice-cream – actually two dishes of it, pink and white – and cake, and fruit, and distracting French bonbons, and in the middle of the table four great bouquets of hot-house flowers!

It quite took their breath away; and they stared first at the table an then at their mother, who looked as if she enjoyed it immensely.

"Is it fairies?" asked Amy.

"It's Santa Claus," said Beth.

"Mother did it"; and Meg smiled her sweetest, in spite of her grey beard and white eyebrows.

"Aunt March had a good fit, and sent the supper," cried Jo, with a sudden inspiration.

"All wrong; old Mr Laurence sent it," replied Mrs March.

RICHMAL CROMPTON

(1890-1969)

Richmal Crompton was the *nom de plume* of Richmal Crompton Lamburn who created one of the most memorable figures in the juvenile fiction of the twentieth century: William Brown. Often known as 'just William' after the title of one of the early books in a collection of 38, William and his 'outlaw' friends have amused generations of avid followers and continue to do so. With his outrageous and often anti-social behaviour in an imaginary genteel, inter-war world of middle class England, William encapsulates intolerance with fussiness and pomposity. His popularity in more recent years has been greatly enhanced by the actor Martin Jarvis in a series of broadcast recordings of his adventures and his exploits have been dramatised for Television. William, who was a particular scourge of fussy little girls and old ladies may seem to be an unusual subject for a writer who, as a girl, frequented a very female world and who later became a leading feminist and a teacher in an all- girls' school. Like Jo, in *Little Women* (a book she admired greatly) Richmal often retreated to the attic in her childhood home in Bury, and there let her imagination rove into writing of all kinds.

We owe much of our knowledge of Richmal Crompton's life to Mary Cadogan's biography: *Richmal Crompton: the woman behind Just William* (1986 and 2003)

Cadogan provided a sympathetic and inspiring picture of a home where learning and the classics were treasured. Her father, with whom Richmal was later to maintain a correspondence in Latin when she went to boarding school, was one of those liberal nineteenth-century clergymen who taught classics and, together with his vivacious wife, created an atmosphere of enjoyment and enrichment. The Rev. Lamburn apparently placed a map of the world in the bathroom and thought nothing of requiring his two daughters and son to sit on the edge of the bath for a geography lesson, and, above all, he instilled in his children a profound knowledge and love of myths and legends from Ancient Greece and Rome..

The first major experience of theatre in Richmal Crompton's life of which we have record is her enthusiasm for school 'theatricals' which are still very much part of the ethos of English Girls' boarding schools. A school magazine for 1907 from Richmal's school, St. Elphins records that:

..we come to another original play by VA, the authoress in this case being Ray Lambourn (the name by which Richmal was known at school). This had not much plot, but was mainly as skit on many school customs and incidents. Ray herself was a most undignified king, who could not possibly keep his accounts, even with the incompetent help of his chancellor (Dorothy Appleyard). There was a princess (Dorothy Birch-Jones) who married a shepherd (Kathleen Thomas,) and a witch in the person on Gladys Wilson.

The same magazine reported that Richmal's older sister, Gwen, had appeared as a 'stalwart Romeo' in the balcony scene of a production by the lower sixth

Inevitably, much later, Richmal Crompton's anti-hero William penetrated the world of Girls' School dramatics with disastrous consequences. In the book *William in Trouble*, a story entitled 'William and the Fairy Daffodil' shows William at his most daring and inventive in imaginative terms.

William has managed to gain access to a Girls' boarding school's grounds and has been taken into an Art class as a model, having been mistaken for the gardener's boy. At the end of the class William finds himself alone with a little girl to whom he tells many 'tall stories':

Suddenly the little girl put down her head on her arms and began to cry. 'Oh, don't,' said William greatly distressed. 'What's the matter? Have you got toothache?'
'No-o!'
'Has anyone been unkind to you?'
'No-o-o-o!'

'Tell me if they have,' he went on threateningly, 'I'll kill 'em for you. I don' mind how many people I kill. I've been where no white man ever-'
'I'm homesick,' wailed the girl. 'I want to go h-o-o-o-me.'
'Well-well, you go home then, ' counselled William encouragingly, almost tenderly, 'you *go* home. I'll *take* you home.'
' I c-c-can't'
'Why not?'
She dried her eyes.
'Well, I'm in a play we're doing this afternoon, and if I don't turn up for it they'll know something's happened, and they'll c-c-catch me before I get to the station ,and bring me b-b-b-back!'
'No, they *won't*, 'said William. 'I-I'll help you. I tell you, no one'll ever dare stop me. I've been where no white man has ever set his feet'an I've had my legs cut off without gas an-'
'Yes,' said the little girl quite unimpressed,' but don't you see I can't go at once 'cause I've not had dinner yet, an' I'm hungry, an' if I run away after dinner they'll find me at once and c-c-c-catch me.'
She burst into sobs again.
'No, don't,' said William desperately. 'Don't cry. It's all right. I'll take care of you. I-I say' –the light of inspiration shone suddenly in his face-
'I'll take your part in the play an' then they'll never know you've gone an'you'll get home all right.'
She stopped crying and gazed at him, then the hope died from her face and she burst into a wail.
'B-b-but you don't look like a fa-a-a-airy,' she sobbed.
'I could *make* myself look like one,' said William grimly, 'I bet I could-
Look-look at me now.'
He gazed into the distance, his features composed into a simper that suggested to an impartial observer a mixture of coyness and imbecility.
'Oh, no-o-o-o! she wailed. 'It doesn't-Oh, *don't!*'
Disappointed, William dismissed the expression which had been meant to represent the faery for which his heart had such a profound contempt.
'Well,' he said, 'if it looks wrong, can't I cover my face with somethin'?'
Her tears ceased. Her eye shone. She clasped her hands.
'Oh, I *forgot!*' she said, 'there's a veil. They won't see your face. Oh, you are a *nice* boy. Will you *rally* do it? Listen, I'll tell you *just* what to do. I'm Fairy Daffodil- I'll get you the clothes in a second. There's a cap

of daffodil petals, and a veil tht comes down from them over your face, so *that's* all right. And you have to hide behind the green bank at the side of the stage behind a lot of green stuff and leaves. Miss Pink and Miss Grace went into the woods in the car this morning to get the green stuff and leaves. You go there early, about two, and then when the others come they'll be so busy getting ready that they won't bother you. I'll leave you the book and you can pretend to be reading, and when it begins you wait there till someone calls 'Fairy Daffodil,' and then you come out and bow and say, 'Here am I-speak, Queen' And when that bit's over you just sit down on the stool by the side of the queen's throne and you don't speak again. It's quite easy. Oh, it is *kind* of you, dear boy.'

William's freckled countenance flamed again.

'Oh, it's nothin' he said modestly, 'It's nothin' to what I'd do for you, and it's nothin' to what I've done. Why, I've been where no white man's ever set his feet before. This is *nothin'* to that An' if they catch you and bring you back,' he gave a short, sinister laugh, 'well, they'd better look out, that's all.'

She gazed at him with bright eyes. 'Oh, it *is* so kind of you. I-I'd go now at once, but I'm so hungry and-and it's treacle-tart today.

****

The guests swarmed into the school hall. In the middle of the second row sat William's father and mother, Mr. and Mrs. Brown. The room was tastefully decorated with leaves and bracken.

'I like to come to all these affairs, don't you?' said the lady next top Mrs. Brown. 'I really didn't want to have big girls' school so near the village, but now it's come it's best to be sociable, and I must say they're always very good about sending out invitations to all their little affairs'.

'Oh, yes,' said Mrs. Brown vaguely, 'and it all looks very nice.'

The curtain rose and the two ladies continued their conversation in a whisper.

'Very pretty,' said Mrs. Brown.

'Isn't it?' said the other. 'Oh, it's quite a nice change to come along to a thing of this sort once in a way-

'Well, I must say,' admitted Mrs. Brown, 'I like to get right away from home sometimes, because really, at home I'm on pins the whole time, not knowing whatever William's going to do next. At a place like this I feel *safe*. It's nice to be anywhere where I *know* that William can't suddenly rise up before my eyes doing something awful.'

'Fairy Daffodil!' called the fairy herald on the stage. A figure arose from behind a leafy barrier, took an ungraceful step forward, tripped over the leafy barrier and crashed to earth-leafy barrier and all. The yellow headgear rolled off on to the floor, revealing a tousled head over a stern, earth-streaked freckled face.

'What's your boy like?' said Mrs. Brown's neighbour, who was not looking at the stage. 'I don't think I've ever seen him'.

But Mrs. Brown's smile had faded. Her face had become a mask of horror. Her mouth had dropped open. Her neighbour followed her eyes to the stage. The strange apparition was in no wise disconcerted by the strange contretemps with the leafy barrier. It did not even trouble to recover its headgear. It stood in the middle of the stage and said loudly and ferociously 'Here I am!-'

There was dead silence. Fairy Bluebell, who stood near, inspired by a gallant British determination to carry on in spite of all disasters, prompted

'Speak-'

William looked at her haughtily. 'I've just spoke,' he said.

'Speak, Queen,' hissed Bluebell desperately.

'It's not my turn,' hissed the Queen back.

Bluebell stamped

'Say, "speak Queen" ' she said to William

'Oh.,' said William, 'I'm sorry. I forgot that bit. I forgot that there was something else. Speak Queen. That's all, anyway, isn't it? Where's the stool?'

He looked round, then calmly sat down on the stool. Sublimely unaware of actors and audience completely paralysed around him.

Slowly, very slowly, the power of speech returned to Mrs. Brown. Her horror-stricken eyes left the stage. She clasped her husband's arm.

'John,' she said hysterically, 'it-it-it's William.'

Mr Brown, too, had gazed open mouthed at this wholly unexpected apparition of his son. Then he recovered himself.

'Er-nonsense, my dear,' he said firmly, 'Never seen the boy before. Do you hear? We've never seen the boy before.'

'B-b-b-but we have, John,' she said. 'It's William!'

'Who's William?' said Mr. Brown wildly.' There isn't any William. Temporarily, I've disowned him. I've disowned him till we meet again under the shelter of our own roof. I don't know how he got here or what he's going to do, and I don't care. He's nothing to do with me. I've disowned him. I tell you-I've disowned him.
'Oh, John,' wailed Mrs. Brown. Isn't it *awful!'*

The situation, of course, plumbs new depths of farce before William is eventually hounded offstage and makes his escape! One can sense the author's personal experience of school plays underpinning the story.
William's stage career reaches its apotheosis in the story 'William Holds the Stage' which appeared in the book *William the Pirate* (1932). A well-meaning but pompous ex pupil of William's school considers himself an expert on the Shakespearean authorship debate and asks to deliver a lecture at the school and inaugurate a Shakespeare Competition. Both have catastrophic and hilarious consequences as William teases out the difference between Bacon and Ham-let and eventually delivers a memorable but excruciatingly inaccurate version of 'to be or not to be'. Again we can almost feel the influence of those house drama competitions and festivals that became established as part of many schools in the early years of the twentieth century and, in some cases, continue to this day.

After her own time at a girls' boarding school Richmal went on to gain a place to read classics at Royal Holloway College, an all-women's college of London University at Egham in Surrey. Significantly, this college now has one of the largest and finest departments of Theatre and Drama in the world and maintains several Professorships. When Richmal Crompton was a student there the seeds of this area of specialism were being sown. Mary Cadogan records that:
There was a great deal of interest in drama, and Richmal's contributions to theatricals was enthusiastic, and the subject of warm appreciation in a testimonial from Margaret Taylor. 'she has contributed to the general amusement by her acting and by her facility in producing occasional verses'. (p.45)

She was, in fact, also secretary to the classical club and secretary and later treasurer of the Christian Union. When her turn came to become a teacher herself, Richmal first returned to her old school, St, Elphin's but then took up a post as classics teacher at Bromley High School in a then leafy and affluent suburban part of Kent (now the London Borough of Bromley). Inevitably, she sought to imbue her pupils with the same passion for classics and theatre that she had acquired and developed. Our next extract demonstrates an interesting symmetry with the piece taken from the St. Elphin's magazine, for Mary Cadogan draws upon the magazine of Bromley High School to illustrate her awareness of Richmal Crompton's enthusiasm:

Her love of classical drama led her to take parties of girls to see performances of *Medea, Alcestis* etc. at a time when the school did not organise many outings, and she also became involved at a practical level in theatricals. A July 1922 issue of the magazine states: 'The Dramatic Society gave two performances of *A Midsummer Night's Dream* at the end of the Summer term 1921. The Society was then on trial as it was its first undertaking. However, thanks to the timely aid of Miss Lamburn during the last week of rehearsals, and the keenness of all concerned-actors, understudies and scene-shifters alike-it was a great success and a considerable sum was raised, which was devoted to school needs…Miss Lamburn has now very kindly become a member of the Committee and its most indefatigable 'coach' and stage manager' (p62)

Richmal wrote about some of these activities a decade later, in 1933, on the occasion of the school's fiftieth anniversary. Incidentally, her memory seems slightly faulty regarding the first play that the dramatic society presented, which was not *As You Like It* but *A Midsummer Night's Dream*.
'The Dramatic Society was originally started by a group of the elder girls. They chose *As you Like It,* assigned the parts, rehearsed it, and had got it well under weigh before they called me in as producer shortly before the performances, in order, I believe, to have someone to blame in case by any unlikely chance the thing turned out a failure. It was far from a failure, and they followed it by excellent performances of *The Rivals, The Merchant of Venice,* and scenes from *Emma.* I don't remember any

contretemps in connection with these except the accidental breaking of plaster cast – I think it was the Venus de Milo-that we had borrowed from the studio without permission , to enhance the effect of a moonlit garden. I confessed this to Miss Richardson on the Monday morning in a state of almost hysterical abjectness and she was very nice about it.'

Richmal Crompton's account of school dramatics has remarkable similarities with what still happens in many boarding schools. There may now be drama teachers and drama studios and one wonders whether the sums of money raised by the productions in Crompton's day went towards such facilities! During her time at Bromley High School, she had begun to write her William books as well as serious novels but, sadly her days as a talented and inspiring teacher were soon to end because she contracted polio and spent the rest of her life as a full-time writer and semi-invalid. Her biographer does not fail to record the consequences for Richmal's love of theatre:

Her taste for theatrical entertainment was something else that now had to be expressed in a less active way; she could no longer be the mainstay of school or church drama groups, but William could continue to put on his plays, tableaux and 'human waxwork' shows in the old barn (even if he could hardly ever manage to extract from the local children who made up his audience the agreed admission charge of a penny or halfpenny). Some of William's theatrical performances were inspired by Richmal's juvenile experiences of acting with Gwen in a church hall in Bury in aid of the Waifs and Strays Society. William, however, seems to have had illusions of grandeur when he is involved in amateur dramatics, even when his role is tiny, or when he is assigned a backstage job. Coerced into helping with sound effects for a production by the local literary society, William hankers for the hero's part so strongly that, when he encounters a distinguished professional trader of the boards he feels justified in speaking to him on equal terms:
'Do you know who I am?' (the stranger said majestically)s
'No' said William simply, 'an' I bet you don't know who I am either.'
'I am a very great actor,' Said the man.
'So 'm I,' said William promptly.

Village theatricals are also featured in some of her adult books, with varying degrees of hilarity. Richmal enjoyed visits to the professional theatre in London with Gwen, and later, with her niece Richmal. She was not especially musical but had a taste for Gilbert and Sullivan, hated jazz and liked to hear classical music on the radio.

C,HENRY WARREN

(b.circa 1900)

Henry Warren became well known as a travel writer, providing elegant depictions of aspects of rural England, but his most enduring work is his autobiographical *A Boy in Kent* (1937) in which he describes life in a Kentish village during the early years of the twentieth century, before the First World War. Warren's village, Mereworth, was situated in the hop-growing area of West Kent and he witnessed the annual migration of East Londoners into his area for the hop harvest. As a son of the local shopkeeper and baker he was also uniquely placed to observe the many 'characters' of the village and he clearly developed a sense of drama because, as an adult, he described many of them in theatrical terms. Henry, for instance, wrote of 'the early morning bakehouse drama' that 'had changed its character for me. George was no longer the sole actor, or, if he was, there remained always the possibility that Flo' might step up and take a part.'

One of the features of village life that Henry noted was the enormous social and economic gulf between the villagers and the inhabitants of the great house nearby. The arrival of 'her ladyship' at any event was moment for awe and respect and her entrance into Church was the cue that the vicar might begin the service. Henry Warren particularly remembered the occasion when the lady, with 'hundreds of years of blue blood in her bearing' mixed with the general populace at closer quarters:

… The occasion was a concert organised to collect funds for the refurbishing of the church, and so perhaps her ladyship felt that here, if ever, was a cause for which she must give, not only money, but herself. With amazement we heard that she was going to attend: the thing was almost unbelievable. And when the evening came, every chair in the decorated schoolroom was taken long before the concert was timed to begin.

Curious and eager, we waited for her ladyship to enter, but there was no sign of her. The first item was announced. Was she going to disappoint us after all? As politely as we could, we listened to some songs and recitations and a solo on the faltering piano, but our heart was in none of them. Then, during a pause, the door opened and her ladyship entered, followed by Miss Mearson carrying a roll of music. The vicar led them to their seats in the front row and while Miss Mearson divested her mistress of her cloak and untied the black lace scarf which she wore over her hair, there was a whispered consultation. Our interest was not lacking now, and when the vicar mounted the platform and told us that her ladyship was going to sing, there was a mighty round of applause.

Pale and lovely she stood on the stage before us, her sequined dress shimmering as she breathed, a cluster of diamonds flashing from her fingers. Miss Mearson played through the opening bars, while with folded hands her ladyship waited, looking over our heads with a gentle smile. Impersonal as that smile was, it kindled us like a benediction. When the prelude was over, and Miss Mearson had given a little nod, we heard her voice, thin and maybe a little cracked, singing the song that was always to be associated with her memory in the future. It would not have mattered to us what she sang; but 'Sally in our Alley' was her choice, and no doubt she had given much thought to it. I for one knew nothing much about alleys, and even less about the Sallies who lived in them, but such ignorance could not hinder our delight.

Such a near view, however, was something that obviously could not be looked for again. We must content ourselves with these Sunday-morning services, when, erect and rustling, she walked up the aisle to her pew. Anything that might happen thereafter, during the course of the service, was bound to be of inferior appeal.

Our second extract is taken from the section entitled 'The Secret Pool' and it provides a magical evocation of the fantasy world of the toy theatre:

One of my most treasured possessions was a toy theatre. It stood about twenty inches high and was something under two feet from back to front. The stage, uprights, and flies were all made of good stout wood, but the remainder of the theatre had been cut out of thick cardboard which time and some rough usage had rendered somewhat frayed and broken. Painted on the proscenium were elegant mermaids splashing about in elegant waves; and at the top of all was a jewelled crown that rested on a cushion of woolly clouds – emblem of who knows what royal patronage?

For the footlights there was a slot across the front of the stage wherein diminutive candles could be fixed with the most dazzling effects; but only on the very rarest occasions was I allowed to indulge this gorgeous display, for fear of fire. And, indeed, one day it nearly happened so. Only the foresight of a young friend in crushing a rug over the whole affair prevented a final conflagration. As it was, my theatre ever after wore in places a smeared and smoky look that would have been distressing to a more professional producer. But for me it was quite without fault: the illusion it provided was so complete that I hardly considered it as a toy. When I had sent up the red-plush curtain (a tricky business, since the pole rested none too securely on a couple of bent pins) the performance that followed lacked little for me, whatever it may have lacked for others.

Nor was I worried overmuch because the play was produced under such considerable difficulties. My sets were limited to three: a woodland scene, a tropical island scene, and a royal palace scene. With these, consisting each of four wings and a backcloth, almost any theme was possible, given a little imagination on the part of the audience; and since the audience usually consisted solely of myself, there was no cavilling when a bead-hung native came on to the stage and began hobnobbing with an ermined noble. My favourite scene was the royal palace, where ample pillars were looped with cloth of gold and scarlet and made glittering with a liberal sprinkling of silver dust; but the tropical island scene, which consisted of palm-trees and a blood-orange sunset over the sea, was a good second. As for the third, perhaps I was too used to woods to care for them on my stage, where all must be as rare and remote as possible.

My players, who numbered several dozens all told, lived only on one side of the cardboard and for this reason were rather restricted in their movements. They fitted tightly (or at least were meant to do so) into little tin sockets soldered onto the end of a stick of wire, and in time I became fairly expert in their difficult manipulation. It was the extra hands, the greenhorns, that gave me all the trouble. Sometimes my plots were so complicated that I felt they called for extra actors and actresses, and these I would cut out and paint for myself. But they always managed to topple over at the most inopportune moments, or else they wilted so badly that I was compelled to remove them from the company.

In the centre of the stage floor there was a small trap-door, which served equally well for a well down which the villain might be dropped, or a dungeon, or a cave out of which the fairy queen could ascend in her tinselled splendour. As for the orchestra, this was painted in permanent full blast below the footlights. Here, too, I sometimes felt constrained to call in aid. For this purpose I made use of an old phonograph which I possessed. But such an asset was accompanied by severe disadvantages. To begin with, it held up the play while I fitted a new cylinder in place. It also offended my sense of the fitness of things by loudly announcing, in a most nasal voice, that this was an Edison Bell R-r-record! In time I dispensed with the phonograph altogether, and tried to find a more suitable substitute by playing *entr'acte* music on the piano. But this proved too complicated, since I was also my own stage-manager and producer, and in the end I was compelled to be content with those unheard melodies from below the footlights.

Indeed, those unheard melodies were really much more appropriate; for my plays were also performed without the aid of the spoken word. An ejaculation here and there, as the plays touched their more emotional peaks, seemed to me all that was necessary; for the rest, the text existed entirely in my own brain. I can understand now that this must have minimised the effect and caused a certain amount of confusion to such audiences as I managed to muster, at a penny a time, and it may well have accounted for their dwindling attention and misplaced laughter; but at the time I did not think it mattered. However others might be affected, I myself had little difficulty in appreciating the performances of my little band of actors, and nothing else really mattered. I did not possess any of those playsheets that were so popular with owners of toy theatres; and, not having even heard of them, I did not miss them. I either invented my own plots or borrowed them from whatever book happened to occupy my mind at the time. If the results of my invention were not as clear to others as to myself, it was not I who was offended thereby.

As a matter of fact, I do not remember that anybody but myself ever took these performances seriously or volunteered anything in the way of constructive criticism. This was my world and I was its only creator and critic. If sometimes others condescended to stoop and peer through the painted proscenium, I allowed them to do so more for the sake of their pennies than for any hope of intelligent praise. But mostly I was left alone with my awkward artistry. Night after night I would clear the big dining-room table and fix up my theatre so that the swinging oil-lamp shone full on to the stage. My mother, sitting over her needlework by the fireside, clearly had no idea of the dramatic masterpieces that were being thrown off so easily a few feet away. Peremptorily, in the midst of one of my most exacting scenes, she would rise and demand a space on the table for some such trivial task as the cutting out of a dress. Or, if it was not my mother, then it was Mary, who came bustling in with the table-cloth and insisted, in a tone of voice that suggested she would sweep the whole bag of tricks into the fire if I did not hurry, on laying the supper. Then I must dissemble the scene as quickly as possible, tumbling the actors off the stage without so much as a hasty curtain to cover their ignominy, and abandon the play for another night.

In my theatre at least, life was as I chose to make it; and now I was beginning to discover a similarly inviolable state of affairs in books and magazines and papers. In a glass-covered book-case that stood in the sitting-room, safe from everyday use, was kept our little stock of books. The book-case was surmounted by a trio of ruby-red vases that towered to a fantastic height and tinkled alarmingly whenever a steam-roller passed down the Street. Opening the doors I would be met by a musty smell that had so deeply permeated the yellowing pages of the books inside that, even if I took them out of doors with me, to read in the summer-house or sprawled upon the grass, the odour remained. But a country boy's reading is mostly done in winter, and so I associate my earliest books with lamp-lit evenings when I lay on the rug before the fire, one hand cupping an aching chin.

MARY (M.V.) HUGHES

(1866-1965)

Mary Vision Hughes is best known for her series of lively memoirs, of which *A London Child in the 1870s* is the first. She stated their purpose as being 'to show that Victorian children did not have such a dull time as is supposed.' In adult life she became a leading Educationalist with profound insights into the needs of young people. Growing up with four brothers, life was always lively, but it seems strange to modern eyes to relate that she was excluded from the many excursions organised for her brothers: she never even saw a Christmas pantomime!

Left to her own devices for much of the time she devised her own imaginative entertainment with the simplest of props.

"While the boys were off, and mother busy, I was completely happy with a wooden stool on four legs, padded with red velvet. It was a treasure belonging to the landlady, who brought it out for me specially, with the request that the young gentlemen should not sit on it. Mother, knowing the young gentlemen, hid it always until they were out of the way, and then I had such glory with it that it compensated for my being left at home. It became in turn a table, a bed, a funeral coach, a train, a station, a pirate vessel for stealing mother's brushes or cotton, and oftenest of all it was Bucephalus, on which I careered about the room, conquering country after country. The boys returned all too soon.

… there was also the curious occupation of cutting patterns in perforated cardboard, sticking them on a piece of coloured ribbon, and inflicting them on some aunts as a Bible bookmark. I had a boyish contempt for dolls, especially the flaxen-haired blue-eyed type, whose clothes wouldn't take off. These came in handy as an audience, for one of my favourite games was to hang over the foot of my bed, and preach to the counterpane, with a text duly given out twice, in different directions.

I must have done this to break the silence. No London child today can realize the quiet of the road on which my window looked. A tradesman's cart, a hawker or a hurdy-gurdy, were the sum total of the usual traffic. Sometimes everything had been so quiet for so long that the sound of a passer-by or of a butcher's pony would take on a distant, unreal tone, as if it were mocking me. This frightened me, and I would break the spell by singing 'The Lass of Richmond Hill'.

Music I made for myself with broken nibs stuck into the edge of my table. The tinkle was cheering, but no tune could I achieve although Charles made effective ones on his 'organ' of nibs.

In spite of my contempt for dolls of the usual kind, and my intense hatred of sewing, I took great delight in dressing up the pawns of a very large set of chess-men, discarded by the family. White pawns became Arthur's knights or Greek heroes, as the fancy took me, black ones were pagans or Trojans. Bright bits of velvet and silk were sewn on them by my toiling fingers, and cardboard swords fitted to their sides. The best bits of stuff and passionate care were expended on Sir Lancelot, who slaughtered pagans with easy grace on my washing stand."

. **The dramatic highlight of the year was the annual Christmas play.**

"Nowadays it is difficult to realize that no Christmas preparations were made until the week before the day itself. All our excitement was packed into a short space. The boys were on holiday, and all over the place. [Mother was mostly in the kitchen, presiding over mincemeat and puddings. I was set to clean currants, squeeze lemons, and cut up candied peel. Barnholt lent a hand at chopping the suet, but kept making raids on the lumps of sugar tucked away in the candied peel, which he assured me were very hard and nasty in the mincemeat, but had no ill effects on him.]

… The afternoons were generally given up to the preparation of our annual play. It fell to Tom to devise the plot, and to Charles, the Bully Bottom of the family, fell nearly everything else. He took the part of the villain or the comic washerwoman, and kept thinking up ideas for improving the parts of the others. He taught me how to act when I wasn't speaking, how to listen with agitation, how to do 'by-play', how to swoon, and once even how to die. Dym was usually the hero, a bit stiff, but always dignified. Barnholt had to be given a part with little to say, because, however willing, he could not be relied on to remember the words, or improvise other ones. What he really loved was to be the policeman, coming in at the crisis with a "'Ere, what's all this?", pulling out his note-book, wetting his thumb, and taking people's addresses. He knew his stuff for this perfectly, but it wouldn't always fit into melodrama.

Tom, to my great comfort, was prompter, and saved me from many a breakdown when I was swamped with nervousness. I didn't actually forget my words, but I should have done if Tom hadn't stood by smiling at me behind the screen.

Christmas Eve was the day we liked best. The morning was a frenzied rush for last rehearsals, last posting of cards, last buying of presents. My father came home early, laden with parcels. The tea-table was resplendent with bon-bons (crackers), sweets, and surprise cakes with icing on the top and threepenny-bits inside.

Then followed the solemn ascent to the study for the play. The boys had borrowed chairs from the bedrooms, and placed them in two rows: the front (stalls) for father, mother, and any aunt, uncle, or visitor who happened to be there, and the back (pit) for the servants, who attended with much gigglement.

Personally I was thankful when this nerve-strain was over, and we all crowded down into the breakfast-parlour. Here, earlier in the day, mother and I had arranged the presents – a little pile for each, and we all fell upon them with delight.

GWEN RAVERAT

(1885-1957)

Gwen Raverat was the granddaughter of the famous naturalist Charles Darwin whose book *The Origin of Species* firmly established the concept of Evolution. Darwin himself was clearly not the stereotypical Victorian father and the family home at Downe in Kent was a place of fun and creativity. This model of childhood as a time for play and adventure influenced Darwin's children and so his son George, who married Maud du Puy, also created a similar environment for his family at their home in Cambridge.

Much later in life, George and Maud's daughter Gwen recreated aspects of her almost magical childhood in her book *Period Piece*, first published in 1956 and remaining in print until this day. The book is beautifully illustrated with Gwen's own evocative line drawings and presents a wonderful company of colourful and sometimes eccentric relations and other characters. She vividly recalls the games and activities of her childhood and these include both theatre visits and plays created at home. Although Gwen is largely remembered as an illustrator the influence of her early experience of theatre enabled her to produce set designs in 1927 for a proposed ballet to be based on William Blake's *Illustration of the book of Job* as a recognition of the centenary of the poet's death. With music by another of Gwen's famous relations, the composer Ralph Vaughan Williams, the work was eventually entitled *Job, a masque for dancing*.

The house to which Gwen Raverat's memories refer is now incorporated into the buildings of Darwin College, Cambridge.

In our first extract, Gwen recalls a very early experience of the live theatre: not, as with many children, a visit to a pantomime or children's play but to the performance of a Greek Tragedy, verse translations of which were slowly becoming popular at the turn of the century.

There is a long letter about a visit to London to see an amateur performance of a Greek play in 'Lady Freak's house' [? Freke]. *At 12 we were all packed, I with my grey dress and red velvet hat on, and lavender dress in a valise – Aunt C. in her best black silk dress, with her Spanish lace dress in her box. We were seated in the cab* [American for railway carriage] *when suddenly I was aroused by Aunt C saying in stentorian tones, 'I have forgotten the tickets for the Greek play.'* After some agitation they *decided to run the risk of being turned away* and went off shopping to *Picadolly* [sic] *and Regent Streets.*

... And then there was *Charley's Aunt*. This was the first real play we ever saw. It did not seem to me at all funny, only tremendous and exciting; and, at one point, most dangerously improper. I have never seen the play since then, but as I remember it, one of the young men dressed up as Charley's Aunt and ran across the stage, lifting up his petticoats and *showing his trousers underneath*. Nothing since then has ever shocked me so much."

Gwen said –

"I had a solitary game of my own, played at bedtime; it was called 'Being Kind to Poor Pamela'. Pamela was a child with whom I sometimes played, but whom I rather despised. The game was played by getting out of bed and lying on the floor, until you were as cold as you could bear to be. During that time you were Poor Pamela, lying out in the snow in her nightgown, owing to the cruelty of her parents. She was starving and the wolves were howling in the woods all round. Then you became yourself again, and went out into the could and rescued poor Pamela – the wolves were getting very near – and you put her into your own bed and warmed her, and fed her, and comforted her most tenderly. This made you feel frightfully good and kind; and you cold do it over and over again, until you could keep awake no longer. On showing this passage to Margaret, she revealed that she had independently practised a variety of this sport, when put to bed with a hot-water bottle, because she had a cold; only it was not Pamela whom she impersonated by lying naked on the oil-cloth, but a mother with a baby (a doll). A good cure for a cold."

In the relaxed environment of their upbringing, the children's creativity flourished:

"I never played with dolls at all, except when they were useful for acting – to be sailors in a ship-wreck, or human sacrifices.

From the far beginnings of dumb crambo and charades, we gradually climbed to the heights of the Christmas play. This was written in Committee, by all of us together, and was the principal event of the year. As soon as one play was acted we instantly began planning the next one, even upon Boxing Day! They were performed in our house, on the evening of Christmas Day, and were followed by the Christmas dinner, which was attended by all the family then in Cambridge, and by no one else at all. But as Downe was nearly always full of aunts and uncles, this wasn't a problem.

These plays were built up on a good solid foundation of Gilbert and Sullivan, and were full of topical allusions. They always had a Chorus, in which we all took part, whenever we were not on the stage in some other capacity, because we were short of actors. Bernard wrote and recited the Prologue, but he was too grown-up to act with us; Erasmus disliked acting and refused to take part. Charles probably disliked it quite as much, but public opinion always compelled him to be the Prince and to wear the beautiful Russian boots – a present from Felix – which were the Prince's insignia, and the glory of our dressing-up box. Nora was considered to be the prettiest of us (to her disgust), so she generally had to be the Princess, which was very dull for her. Ruth and Margaret were celebrated actresses and had character parts; and the rest of us were Witches, Professors, Ghosts or whatever was required. I did a good deal of the costume designing, and used to cut out dresses by the simple process of laying the patient down on a piece of butter muslin, and cutting out round his edges. But we had a pretty good stock of curious cast-off odds and ends to fall back on. There was no scenery, and only a screen for a curtain. The plots were incredibly complicated; no one really understood them; but that was no matter; for the success of the play depended entirely on the wit, and the verses. The dialogue was in prose, and full of jokes; the verses were mostly written by Ruth and Frances. Here is the opening chorus of *The Magic Snowboot*, which was written when Nora, Frances and I were round about thirteen and fourteen. It was spoken by a *Chorus of the Cooks* of the Princess Lavinia Plantagenet:

THOMAS: You must know our situation
            Is the highest in the nation;
            On a close examination

ALL: Of a heraldry book,

THOMAS: You'll find there's not a badge in it
            So noble as Plantagenet;
            And though you won't imagine it,

ALL: I am that household's cook.

THOMAS: So we cook and wash the crockery,
            Go out and weed the rockery;
            This service is no mockery,

ALL: You probably infer;

THOMAS: Yet we condescend to dish-up
            For a baron or a bishop,
            And we'll sometimes send the fish up

ALL: For an ordinary Sir.

Once the play had to be put off, because we all had influenza and the aunts were in a terrible Darwin fuss about it, which annoyed and shamed us very much. When the play was finally acted, Bernard's Prologue contained these lines:

Fell Influenza, stalking through the land,

From this devoted house has held its hand.
See how each Mother, with a touching pride,
Lays the well-worn thermometer aside.
No less than seven Darwins, be it said,
Are simultaneously out of bed!

Bernard used to write whole plays for use, too. There was *The Apterix* and *The Bishop of South-West Equatorial Mesopotamia*. This last was a summer play, to be acted in the garden …

As we grew older the plays grew more informal, but we still always acted some half-impromptu skit on Christmas Day. The year that Frances got engaged to Francis Cornford, I wrote the play myself: *The Importance of being Frank*. In this all the characters were called Francis or Frances, which caused great confusion, until the hero allowed himself to be called Frank; a solution which the Cornfords did not adopt in real life.

I believe this was the last of the regular plays; after that we got married or turned our attentions to other diversions.

HUGH WALPOLE

(1884-1941)

Hugh Walpole was born in New Zealand but educated in various English boarding schools and at the King's School, Canterbury (an experience which almost certainly contributed to his novel *The Cathedral* that was subsequently dramatised).

He went on to Cambridge University where his literary ability began to flourish. Poor eyesight exempted him from military service, but he worked for the Red Cross and he drew on this wartime activity in his later novels *Dark Forest* and *The Secret City.*

Walpole became a prolific author and, in addition to plays, novels, literary criticism and biography he collaborated with J.B.Priestley, another leading novelist and dramatist, on a novel based entirely on letters: *Farthing Hall.*

Walpole was knighted for his services to the arts in 1937 having been a best-selling novelist with a reputation for vivid plots and scene setting. He was clearly captivated by the idea of theatre and this is demonstrated in a volume from his most successful series of books about his popular creation, Jeremy set in Polchester, Glebeshire.

In this extract from *Jeremy*(1919) the protagonist has his first experience of live theatre: a Christmas pantomime to which he is taken by his much –loved Uncle Samuel

Uncle Samuel paused at a lighted hole in the wall and spoke to a large lady in black silk, who was drinking a cup of tea. Jeremy caught the jingle of money. Then they moved forward, stumbling in the dark up a number of stone steps, pushing at a heavy black curtain, then suddenly bathed in a bewildering glow of scent, light and colour.

Jeremy's first impression, as he fell into this new world, was of an ugly, harsh but funny voice crying out very loudly indeed: "Oh, my great aunt! Oh, my great aunt!" A roar of laughter rose about him, almost lifting him off his feet, and close to his ear a Glebeshire voice sobbed: "Eh, my dear. Poor worm! Poor worm!"

He was aware then that about him on every side gas was sizzling, and then as he recovered slowly his breath, his gaze was drawn to the great blaze of light in the distance, against which figures were dimly moving, and from the heart of which the strange voice came. He heard a woman's voice, then more voices together; then suddenly the whole scene shifted into focus, his eyes were tied to the light; the oranges and the gas and the smell of clothes and heated bodies slipped back into distance – he was caught into the world where he had longed to be.

He saw that it was a shop – and he loved shops. His heart beat thickly as his eyes travelled up and up over the rows and rows of shelves; here were bales of cloth, red and green and blue; carpets from the East, table covers, sheets and blankets. Behind the long yellow counters young men in strange clothes were standing. In the middle of the scene was a funny old woman, her hat tumbling off her head, her shabby skirt dragging, large boots and a red nose. It was from this strange creature that the deep ugly voice proceeded. She had, this old woman, a number of bales of cloth under her arms, and she tried to carry them all, but one slipped, then another, and another; she bent to pick them up and her hat fell off. She reached for her hat and all the bales tumbled together. Jeremy began to laugh – everyone laughed; the strange voice came again and again, lamenting, bewailing, she had secured one bale and a smile of cautious triumph began to spread over her ugly face, then the bales all fell again, and once more she was on her knees. … It was then that her voice or some movement brought to Jeremy's eyes so vividly the figure of their old gardener, Jordan, that he turned round to Uncle Samuel, and suddenly grasping that gentleman's fat thigh, exclaimed convulsively: "why, she's a man!"

JIM HOWLAND

(1919-2009)

Jim was brought up and lived in Wheelwright House, in the Kentish village of Boughton, near Faversham and his life is described in his self-published autobiography *Memories: A Journey through Time* (1988). Jim's life and experience is probably typical of many of his generation and we dwell on it in some detail here.

When mechanisation made the job of wheelwright redundant Jim's father became a greengrocer and Jim helped him on his round from a very early age He sang in the Church choir and this first experience of 'performing' was to stand him in good stead later in life as did his wide experience with cows and his ability to drive!

In the Second World War Jim, 'ginger' Howland served in the $4^{th}/5^{th}$ Buffs Regiment and was captured in Belgium in 1940 whilst holding back the German advance during the evacuation of Dunkirk. He was Prisoner of War in Poland until 1945 and endured horrific experiences which were vividly described by one of his comrades, K.Mc Phail in his poem *Fort 17 in Memory of Five Years of Hell.*.

 His health deteriorated seriously and he had many spells in a so-called 'hospital' but 'performance' brought some relief:

It was just after this that I was asked if I would participate in the POW concert along with another half dozen chaps. We had quite a few laughs at rehearsals. It was a variety show, in which I took the part of the leading lady, some of the parts were a little blue in nature. I know the night of the actual show some of the doctors walked out, but I did notice the Germans stayed and really enjoyed it. As a point of interest I have still got the actual programme of the show

After the war ended Jim, like so many of his contemporaries, had a difficult period of readjustment to civilian life. His father died soon after his 'demob' and he became the sole bread winner.

His first job was to assist the local milkman, delivering in all weathers to outlying villages and supplementing this with window-cleaning. However, this somewhat Spartan and dreary existence was enlivened by his first experiences of amateur drama:

At the village of Sheldwich, I called on a woman who ran an amateur dramatic society, her being the producer. During a conversation with her one day, I became quite interested, it didn't need an awful lot of persuasion from her to make me feel that I wouldn't mind perhaps having a go.

Possibly the fact that I took part in an all male cast concert, during the period that I spent in hospital whilst I was a prisoner of war influenced my decision. In it I took part as a leading lady, obviously, this particular concert was somewhat cruder, than the one I had contemplated taking part in now. Probably because I hadn't got a bad voice, due to singing in the choir as a lad, added as an additional interest and if it provided a bit of fun by being involved, so well and good. According to what developed in the ensuing events I was not likely to be disappointed.

My first attempt on the stage resulted in me having to open the show with a solo taken from one of the London shows, which was, to the best of my knowledge, 'an awful lot of coffee in Brazil'. Now, remembering lines from songs was not one of my good points, consequently, halfway through the song I forgot the words and had to get down from the stage and go over to the pianist to check the rest of the words, then getting back on the stage and carrying on with the song, contrary to what one would think, this produced a huge burst of applause from the audience. I suppose once upon a time I would have been embarrassed, but as I was doing it for the fun of it, I got as much enjoyment out of it.

At another occasion, the lighting was provided by hurricane lamps on the stage, and unfortunately at the spot where I was singing happened to be beneath one that kept dripping oil all of the time, causing me to pay more attention to that than to my vocal pursuits.

Likewise at another village the curtain fell on the whole cast whilst in production, causing a serious scene to be turned into a humorous one, to the delight of the audience, of course. Probably one of the best ones I recall was at Pluckley (the darling buds of May) where one particular scene was taken from a London show, which involved 'the dance of the toy soldiers'.

It required the whole cast dancing around in a circle. At the end of the piece of music, then everyone falls to the floor together. Which was all very well, except for one lady who, unfortunately was rather overweight, and was consequently late in dropping to the floor, causing everyone else to jump up in a cloud of dust, not quite the reaction intended, but never the less all taken in good fun.

Bearing in mind that all these shows were put on to provide entertainment to the villagers and to help charities. There was one show that I remember, where I was required to take part in a love scene, and the lady who played opposite me was a member of the Salvation Army. Now with all due respect to the salvation army, romantic events were not exactly encouraged in those days, with the results that the particular love scene didn't quite come up to expectation according to the producer.

Not knowing who to blame for the lack of fervour, so when the rehearsal was over, the producer suggested to me and my partner that we should spend an evening together in an attempt to enhance our zero performance on the stage. This was all very well, but the problem was that I called on her parents on my milk round, and judging by the reception I received next morning from her mother, one could imagine that all kinds of things had gone on.

Somehow the seriousness of performance ability never did really sink home to me, I always saw the funny side of situations, and made a comedy out of a drama. I suppose it was inevitable that the day came when I was asked not to bother to attend anymore. I put it all down to another passage in my life, which had created a well-earned period of amusement and interest that had been lacking in the past.

Jim concluded his moving if unsophisticated autobiography with these words:

So my life has been full to the brim, poor times, sad times, good times and happy times. On that note, remember, it's your life, one chance, make the most of the things you care for and the people you love and be happy.

EDITH OLIVER

(1872-1948)

Edith Oliver was an English writer of fiction and biography during the period 1927-1951 and she also published her autobiography *Without Knowing Mr. Walkey* in 1938. She was a 'society' lady and photographic portraits of her in the National Portrait Gallery show her in the company of such leading socialites as Lady Ottoline Morrell, Lady Janet Lyte Bailey and members of the Sassoon family.

Her book *Night Thoughts of a Country Lady*(1945) takes the form of the diary of an unnamed character who, we might suspect, has many of her own experiences.

The book, which is:
Dedicated to 'the stranger within my gates', with witty illustrations by Rex Whistler describes its heroine in the following terms:

> She was one of those cultivated and "country" old ladies to be met with in most villages – supremely interested in local affairs, generous to the poor, stern to the evil doer, pardoning to the penitent. She was a leading spirit in all local activities – Church Council, Conservative Association, Women's Institute, Girls' Friendly, and Brownies. She also 'lived her own life', as they say, for she did not consider herself to be altogether of the village. She had moved in wider circles. Her father had been a well-known writer in his day, and his friends had been distinguished people. George Du Maurier was Emma's godfather, and, on her drawing–room wall, there still hung a pen and ink sketch of her as a little girl signed by the famous *Punch* artist. During the summer Miss Nightingale still entertained at week-ends, in the little house put at her disposal by the Squire, those of her friends of her youth who were alive. She was not well off, but she had never thought of taking in 'Paying Guests', and only a European War could have driven her to such a revolution

Yet when the war drove her to fill her house with strange guests, it also drove her to fill her diary with strange thoughts. For the first time in her life, she did not merely enter the names of her guests. She wrote down who they were, why they had come to her house, what they were doing, and how they behaved themselves; for these seemed to be the most extraordinary things about them.

We then read of the Lady's skill in organising various 'cultural and entertainment' activities.

During a recent "Salvage Week" in our district, Miss Nightingale arrived one afternoon in my house, bent down beneath the burden of between fifty and sixty large cloth-bound exercise-books.

"Here is some very good salvage," she said.

"Can you part with them?" I asked. 'Aren't they valuable for reference?"

"Not now, I think. Everything is changing so much that we never need to refer to the past. It doesn't apply."

"It doesn't apply now," she repeated in a sad voice. "The last three years are the only ones that count."

I never saw her again. The next morning, the whole village was shocked by the news that Miss Nightingale had died suddenly in the night. Perhaps I was less surprised than anyone. I had been troubled all the evening by that last glimpse of her when she left her diaries behind at my house. It seemed that she had consciously made an end.

I decided to interpret her last words to me, as making me, in some measure, her literary executor. I carefully read all the volumes through, remembering that she had trusted me to deal with them as I thought best, and now I felt that she had said the true word about her diary.

"It doesn't apply. The last three years are the only ones that count."

I believe that in their new form the diaries do "apply". They give a picture of one aspect of rural life which during the war came into being in many country places – I mean the effect upon them of the influx of strangers in their midst.

In the first few months of the war, one problem faced all of us, who had, either perforce, or of our own free will, become land-ladies – I mean the problem of amusing our guests. We soon saw that the visitors, mostly people from the towns, found country life very dull; and we saw that it was essential to find some occasional outlet for the strangers within our gates. The close quarters were too close.

Every kind of person in the village had some idea of what it meant to give a big party, and to keep that party going. I believe that every village was tackling this job and most of them did really well; but what struck me about it was that we found ourselves, for the first time, mutually responsible for the happiness and welfare of strangers in our neighbourhood.

The parties were our apprenticeship in the art of entertaining strangers, but bigger things were to follow. The village made friends with the men of a Yeomanry regiment from an adjoining county who had been sent here for training, and we decided to organise a weekly dance for them. One difficulty faced us at the start – how should we find partners in the village to balance this large influx of the male sex? One of the organisers explained to me in some anxiety:

"We haven't got nearly enough loose girls, we must import some."

I am a life member of all the local Moral Improvement Societies for the benefit of the young, and in the name of all of them I rose to protest against this importation. I then learnt that the word "loose" related to the proportion of women in our village, and had no moral significance. I withdrew my opposition.

We accordingly invited a bus-load of girls from a neighbouring place to give the required balance to our dance, and I watched, with some interest, the arrival of the "loose girls".

They entered in the huddled and close formation of a swarm of bees, and in that formation they seated themselves well apart from the men. Here they murmured together, like the bees which they resembled in appearance. I cold not think how we could effect the desired fusion between the two sections of our guests. But I had counted without our Master of the Ceremonies. He was a sergeant major, with the winged feet of Mercury, the social tact of Beau Nash, and the gift of imparting the lumpiest partner something of his own grace of movement. With an airy tread he now floated to the middle of the ballroom and called on the gentlemen to Take their Partners. If any gentleman seemed laggard (and many did) he led them to the now well awake and buzzing swarm of loose girls, and made personal introductions. The most alert and attractive of the girls were soon paired off, but there remained a substantial residue who looked heavy. Our Mercury was not deterred. He swung himself into the fray, and danced a few rounds with each of the un-partnered girls. They at once seemed to be the most graceful dancers of all, and as the M.C relinquished each one in turn, she was at once snapped up by a fresh partner. This mercurial man made all our dances the most brilliant successes.

These dances were interspersed with first-rate concerts which were particularly enjoyable to us amateur land-ladies for, besides hearing some very good music, we were asked to put up the distinguished artists who came from London. The first of these concerts might be described as an "All Star" one, and for us country people, it was a new experience to have in our houses those well-known favourites of London audiences. We were extremely proud. Beatrice Lillie proved to be, both on the stage and off, as gay as a lark and most wilfully charming. I had feared that her very sophisticated talent might not go down with these country yeomen, but I could not have been more mistaken. When she stepped on to the stage, and threw round the room one of her demure glances, she captured the audience without singing or saying a word.

After the concert, the visiting artistes, with their hosts and hostesses, met some of the officers at a supper party, and, for those of us who were lucky enough to be invited, this was quite as amusing as the entertainment itself. It was like those suppers on the stage which we read of in the days of Beerbohm Tree. And now we were there. No real supper on the stage could have been more enjoyable.

About Christmas we embarked on our most ambitious attempt in military entertainment. This was a pantomime written, produced and played by local amateurs with a little professional help. It turned out a great success, which was surprising, as it fell a victim, in succession, to every contretemps which is supposed to befall amateur theatricals.

First of all, the company looked on rehearsal as a rather amusing way of spending an hour or two, if there was nothing better to do. The accompanist alone never failed. She accompanied with a complete efficiency, whether or not there was anyone to accompany. Those members of the cast who did sometimes appear, immediately seated themselves in remote corners of the room, there to finish the secret conversations which had begun outside. When the producer succeeded in luring them from these retreats, nearly everyone had first of all to explain, that he or she was not that day playing his or her own part, but was "reading" for an absentee. The patience of the producer proved that this virtue is a supernatural gift of the spirit; but on the one occasion when it did break down, the terror he spread among his flock, and their subsequent good behaviour (which lasted more than one day) proved that he ought really to have been in a fury all the time.

Even when the first night arrived, we found that the whole company had never before met on the stage. And on that occasion, our Pantomime Queen was "down" with an attack of laryngitis which eventually seized, in turns, practically the whole company.

Terrific quarrels developed behind the scenes. Some of the performers had to be coaxed on to the stage in a manner which I believe is sometimes adopted with performing dogs – by holding out a biscuit to create the dramatic bound from the wings. Our "biscuits" were extremely complimentary remarks which we said we had overheard in the audience about the acting of this or that player who had considered slighted on the stage. The feuds which now began were declared by the participators to be eternally incurable, though I believe they were forgotten as soon as the pantomime ended.

Yet none of this drama was guessed at by the spectators; and from the other side of the footlights the whole thing looked rollicking fun. But during those strenuous weeks I saw why it was that one of the most successful theatrical entertainments of my youth had been called "*A Pantomime Rehearsal*".

Our pantomime was not only played for our own regiment, but it travelled to all the neighbouring camps, and then was played under the patronage of the mayors of several seaside resorts, at last actually reaching London. Indeed its run lasted until nearly Easter.

TOM WAKEFIELD

(1935-1996)

Tom Wakefield was born into a mining family in the Midlands in 1935. Money was always scarce, especially when his father was injured at work. While he was recuperating the whole family had to live on "box" money of £2 a week. However, this gave Tom a chance to get to know his father, as the pair went on long walks together in school holidays, and this engendered an affection that was to last all his life. Tom's recollections are documented in his book *Forties' Child – an early autobiography* (1980, Serpent's Tail.)

The *Guardian* described it as "a tender and original recollection of the way a child puts the world together".

When the financial situation eased a little, father proudly booked a holiday with a landlady in Blackpool, and this gave the family their first taste of live entertainment, opening up a whole new world

My father went through our future evenings by holding a finger up each time he announced what was in store for us.

"On Monday night, it's Variety, we'll see Dorothy Squires at the Grand Theatre. She's got a good strong voice, her husband's the pianist, yer know, and he writes the songs. On Tuesday we're going to the circus at the Tower, famous throughout the world Blackpool Tower Circus is – did yer know that?" He did not expect an answer, but held up a third finger.

"On Wednesday, it's George Formby at The Opera House, they say it's a spectackler show. On Thursday we're seeing the show here on the Pier, it's Donald Peers."

"Oh, I like him," said my mother.

"And on Friday we are watching a play. Not listening to one our Tom, like you listen to *Saturday Night Theatre* on the wireless, but watching one, with live actresses and actors."

"Do we want to watch a play?" my mother asked him. I realised he had booked this one specially for me. His answer was clever.

"It's Wilfred Pickles, you know, *Have a Go* on the wireless. Well, he's in a play. *Hobson's Choice*, that's the name of the play. It's a comedy.

"That means it's funny," I said.

"We know what it means, thanks, when we don't we'll ask." My mother was not sharp but she did have an aversion to me if I chose to display any particular intelligence or knowledge that she thought was beyond my age.

Our landlady, Mrs Badger, as well as being kind, was a discreet lady. We had been to the theatre; Dorothy Squire's singing had made my mother cry. This meant that my mother had enjoyed the performance..

JOHN GIELGUD

(1904-2000)

From a modest beginning of convivial family enterprises John Gielgud was to become an almost legendary classical actor, and a celebrated and much-loved director, in spite of his famous gaffs and his tendency to frequently change his mind. He also ran companies, mounting whole seasons in the West End in the 1930s and 40s and continued to direct for many years, maintaining an interest in design, which kept his productions visually interesting.

In 1957 he gave the first performance of *Ages of Man*: his solo performance of a substantial devised Shakespeare recital and for the next ten years he performed it in sixteen countries, gaining fresh recognition as the supreme speaker of Shakespeare's verse.

In the 1960s and 70s, however, he reinvented himself by appearing in the work of new playwrights such as Thornton Wilder, Edward Albee, Peter Shaffer and Alan Bennett for whom he appeared memorably as the Headmaster in *40 Years On.* In 1966 he appeared with Ralph Richardson in David Storey's *Home,* creating a magical partnership for which they were jointly named as 'Best Actors' in the *Evening Standard's* awards. Gielgud replicated this partnership with equal success in Pinter's *No Man's Land* and, by so doing became part of the avant-garde of which he had always been deeply suspicious.

In addition to his stage work, Johnny G, as he was affectionately known, launched himself as a film actor on 1968, playing Lord Raglan in *The Charge of the Light Brigade* and achieved huge personal success playing Henry IV in *Chimes at Midnight* for Orson Welles, with whom he developed a warm working relationship. His final film appearance was in Derek Jarman's remarkable *Prospero's Books* but he will also be remembered for his extraordinary and understated portrayal of Edward Ryder in the television adaptation of Evelyn Waugh's *Brideshead Revisited.*

John was born into the Terry theatrical dynasty, the most celebrated of whom was his aunt Ellen Terry, who he loved dearly.

Like several other individuals featured in this book, Gielgud's early experience included *Peter Pan*. The following is an extract from his early Autobiography, *Early Stages* (1939):

The first play I ever saw was *Peter Pan*, when I was seven. My parents caused me agonies by arriving late. Even now, I cannot bear to miss the beginning of a play. I still love to see the curtain glow as the footlights come up, and to hear the first notes of the orchestra – always provided there is an orchestra. Once, during the War when I was about thirteen years old, my brother came home on leave, and we had a big party at the Gobelins Restaurant, which was fashionable then, for lunch and a matinee of *The Bing Boys on Broadway*. I dismayed the party by making a scene when I saw from the clock that we were twenty minutes late for the performance. When I went to the theatre with Grandmother, we nearly always sat in a box, and I would see the principal actors specially bowing to her when they took their calls. The management would send us tea in the interval, and often we would go round behind and meet the leading actors in their dressing-rooms. Grandmother was a wonderful audience. She laughed and cried whole-heartedly in the theatre, and I naturally did the same.

Sometimes Grandmother would take me to see Fred and Marion and Ellen act. How excited I used to be when I was taken to a theatre where one of them was appearing! I saw Marion in a play called *Wonderful James*. She played the wife of a penniless adventurer who posed as a wealthy man, and in the first act they came together to some business-office. Marion swept in, very dignified, in a grey velvet cloak with ospreys in her hat. Biscuits and port were brought in, and she went on talking grandly, furtively dropping biscuits into her handbag all the time. Later in the play she had a very funny scene in which she sat working a sewing machine, with an overall over her smart dress, murmuring sadly, "Nothing in the larder but half a chicken and a bit of tinned tongue!" I saw her play Mrs Higgins in Shaw's *Pygmalion* with Mrs Patrick Campbell and in *Reparation* at the St. James's with Henry Ainley.

54

Fred Terry and his lovely wife, Julia Neilson, were my idols of course. I saw them first together on the stage in *Sweet Nell*, at which we arrived late. Julia looked up from her orange-basket immediately, and threw a dazzling smile in the direction of our box. On another evening I was taken down to the Boro' Theatre, Stratford, now, alas, no more, to see *The Scarlet Pimpernel*. After the play I went round to the stage door. It was a dark foggy evening. Uncle Fred came out on to the step in all the glory of his white satin and lace, and pressed a sovereign into my hand, like some dandified deity from Olympus.

*

By this time I was deep in dressing up, charades and acting games of all kinds. I was about eight or nine years old. I was not yet stage-struck in the sense of wanting to go on the stage, and I am not conscious of any moment when I suddenly sat up and said "I am going to be an actor". But I see now that my Terry instinct to act was pretty strong from the beginning, though I did not recognise it at the time.

When I was recovering from some disease or other, jaundice or chicken-pox, I forget which, I developed a passion for painting backcloths and designs in pastel for my toy theatre. The colours, in spite of liberal applications of "Fixatif", which smelt like pear-drops, would blow about all over the room and make chalky smears everywhere. I used to prop my cardboard scenery on the mantelpiece and get up in the middle of the night and turn on the light to look at it. (Already I had the stage illusion that everything looks twice as good by artificial light.)

My eldest brother Lewis was at Eton, and there were three of us upstairs in the nursery, my sister Eleanor, my brother Val and myself. We began our stage enterprises with a model theatre – an inspiring affair of cream and gold with a red velvet curtain given me as a birthday present by Mother. We all made up plays and took turns in performing them, standing behind the theatre, and moving the leaden figures about with our hands which were plainly seen by the audience. Cardboard figures with wires were too flimsy and difficult to manage, and in the strangely unquestioning manner of children we accepted the giant's hands moving about in every scene, and simply ignored their existence. Val was responsible for most of the plots and dialogue, and I used to paint the scenery. I had a very strong feeling for space and colour on the stage from the first, and the fascination of scenery, costume and pictorial illusion has never left me. As a child I had no real talent in this direction or I should certainly have become a scenic designer and not an actor at all, but in those days it was the scenery first and the play afterwards so far as I was concerned

WILLIAM SHAKESPEARE

(1564-1616)

We can only speculate how the most famous of all playwrights gained his first experiences of theatre but whoever wrote the plays that are attributed to him clearly enjoyed a classical education and would have been introduced to Greek and Roman drama at a comparatively young age. He would almost certainly have seen performances of Mystery Plays and been aware of some of the traditional folk plays that were popular in rural communities. At some stage he would have been involved with writing roles for boys actors who played the women's roles in Elizabethan theatres and he would seen local actors attempting to grasp the conventions of drama.

Although we have concentrated largely on childhood experiences in this book we felt it was essential to include Shakespeare's memorable picture of amateurs encountering the tasks of acting and putting on plays for the first time provided in his play *A Midsummer Night's Dream.*

Rather misguidedly, perhaps, many teachers have introduced children to Shakespeare through this play because, on the surface, it contains 'suitable' material with its evocation of the fairy world. However, although it is charming to have children representing fairies and other immortals, the play explores themes of adult love and the pretensions and shortcoming of amateur actors.

The play is set in Ancient Athens although the details have remarkable similarities with Elizabethan England. The celebrations of the marriage of Duke Theseus and the Amazon Queen, Hippolyta are in progress and, as part of these celebrations a group of working men have decided to put on a play under the guidance of Peter Quince, who has obviously had some experience of acting and, in the convention of Elizabethan theatre, owns the only copy of the play. The group of workers are often known as the 'mechanicals'; and their names reflect their trades: Quince (from quoins or quines), wooden wedges used in building; Snout, the spout of a kettle; Snug, for the tightness of a joint needed in carpentry; Bottom, for the reel of thread used in weaving; Flute, the sound made by a leaking bellows of a church organ and Starveling, after the proverbial thinness of tailors. Bottom, rather like Just William, imagines that he can play any part and clearly has some flair for histrionics.

This unlikely group of thespians meet at an unspecified location for their first encounter with their play.

Act 1 Sc. 2.

Enter Quince the carpenter, and Snug the joiner, and Bottom the weaver, and Flute the bellows mender, and Snout the tinker, and Starveling the tailor.

QUINCE: Is all our company here?

BOTTOM: You were best to call them generally, man by man, according to the scrip.

QUINCE: Here is the scroll of every man's name which is thought fit through all Athens to play in our interlude before the Duke and Duchess on his wedding day at night.

BOTTOM: First, good Peter Quince, say what the play treats on; then read the names of the actors; and so grow to a point.

QUINCE: Marry, our play is *The Most Lamentable Comedy and Most Cruel Death of Pryamus and Thisbe.*

BOTTOM: A very good piece of work, I assure you, and a merry. Now, good Peter Quince, call forth your actors by the scroll. Masters, spread yourselves.

QUINCE: Answer as I call you. Nick Bottom, the weaver?

BOTTOM: Ready! Name what part I am for, and proceed.

QUINCE: You, Nick Bottom, are set down for Pyramus.

BOTTOM: What is Pryamus? – a lover or a tyrant?

QUINCE: A lover that kills himself, most gallant, for love.

BOTTOM: That will ask some tears in the true performing of it. If I do it, let the audience look to their eyes! I will move storms; I will condole in some measure. To the rest, - Yet my chief humour is for a tyrant. I could play Ercles rarely, or a part to tear a cat in to make all split:

> 'The raging rocks
> And shivering shocks
> Shall break the locks
> Of prison gates,
> And Phibbus' car
> Shall shine from far,
> And make and mar

The foolish fates.

This was lofty! – now name the rest of the players. – this is Ercles' vein, a tyrant's vein; a lover is more condoling.

QUINCE: Frances Flute, the bellows-mender?

FLUTE: Here, Peter Quince.

QUINCE: Flute, you must take Thisbe on you.

FLUTE: What is Thisbe? – a wandering knight?

QUINCE: It is the lady that Pyramus must love.

FLUTE: Nay, faith, let me not play a woman – I have a beard coming.

QUINCE: That's all one: you shall play it in a mask, and you may speak as small as you will.

BOTTOM: An I may hide my face, let me play Thisbe too. I'll speak in a monstrous little voice: 'Thisne, Thisne!' 'Ah, Pyramus, my lover dear! Thy Thisbe dear, and lady dear!'

QUINCE: No, no; you must play Pyramus; and, Flute, you Thisbe.

BOTTOM: Well, proceed.

QUINCE: Robin Starveling, the tailor?

STARVELING: Here, Peter Quince.

QUINCE: Robin Starveling, you must play Thisbe's mother. Tom Snout, the tinker?

SNOUT: Here, Peter Quince.

QUINCE: You, Pyramus' father; myself, Thisbe's father; Snug, the joiner, you the lion's part; and I hope here is a play fitted.

SNUG: Have you the lion's part written? Pray you, if it be, give it me; for I am slow of study.

QUINCE: You may do it extempore; for it is nothing but roaring.

BOTTOM: Let me play the lion too. I will roar that I will do any man's heart good to hear me. I will roar that I will make the Duke say, 'let him roar again, let him roar again'.

QUINCE: An you should do it too terribly you would fright the Duchess and the ladies that they would shriek; and that were enough to hang us all.

ALL: That would hang us, every mother's son.

BOTTOM: I grant you, friends, if you should fright the ladies out of their wits they would have no more discretion but to hang us. But I will aggravate my voice so that I will roar you as gently as any sucking dove. I will roar you and 'twer any nightingale.

QUINCE: You can play no part but Pyramus; for Pyramus is a sweet-faced man; a proper man as one shall see in a summer's day; a most lovely, gentleman-like man. Therefore you must needs play Pyramus.
BOTTOM: Well, I will undertake it. What beard were I best to play it in?
QUINCE: Why, what you will.
BOTTOM: I will discharge it in either your straw-coloured beard, your orange tawny beard, your purple in-grain beard, your perfect yellow.
QUINCE: Some of your French crowns have no hair at all; and then you will play bare-faced! But, masters, here are your parts, and I am to entreat you, request you, and desire you to con them by tomorrow night, and meet me in the palace wood a mile without the town, by moonlight. There will we rehearse; for if we meet in the city we shall be dogged with company, and our device is known. In the meantime I will draw a bill of properties such as our play wants. I pray you, fail me not.
BOTTOM: We will meet, and there we may rehearse most obscenely and courageously. Take pains, be perfect. Adieu!
QUINCE: At the Duke's oak we meet.
BOTTOM: Enough; hold or cut bow-strings.

Exeunt

We see the 'mechanicals' again in Act III, when they have met in a clearing in the woods for their next rehearsal. In this scene much of the humour derives from the fact that the cast is unaware of the conventions of theatre and allow 'reality' and 'illusion' to become hopelessly confused. It is, of course, precisely the ability to create drama through the imagination that characterises so much play and theatre in childhood.

Oberon, the King of the Fairies, has put a spell on his Queen, Titania, in a fit of jealousy, so that she will fall in love with the first person she sees when she awakes from sleep. Inevitably, she is awoken by Bottom as he struts around singing! The incongruous scene of love which follows, involving a company of fairies, has been a favourite of generations of young people and, in addition to providing material for school drama, has sometimes been played by well-known comedians. Our next extract shows the rustic actors struggling with the conventions of Theatre and this short scene precedes the events we have described above.

Act III Sc. 1.

Enter the clowns: QUINCE, BOTTOM, SNUG, FLUTE, SNOUT, *and* STARVELING.
BOTTOM: Are we all met?
QUINCE: Pat, pat; and here's a marvellous convenient place for our rehearsal. This green plot shall be our stage, this hawthorn brake our tiring-house, and we will do it in action as we will do it before the Duke.
BOTTOM: Peter Quince!
QUINCE: What sayest thou bully Bottom?
BOTTOM: There are things in this comedy of Pyramus and Thisbe that will never please. First, Pyramus must draw a sword to kill himself, which the ladies cannot abide. How answer you that?
SNOUT: By'r lakin, a parlous fear!
STARVELING: I believe we must leave the killing out, when all is done.
BOTTOM: Not a whit. I have a device to make all well. Write me a prologue, and let the prologue seem to say we will do no harm with our swords, and that Pyramus is not killed indeed; and for the more better assurance, tell them that I, Pyramus, am not Pyramus, but Bottom the weaver. This will put them out of fear.
QUINCE: Well, we will have such a prologue, and it shall be written in eight and six.
BOTTOM: No, make it two more; let it be written in eight and eight.
SNOUT: Will not the ladies be afeard of the lion?
STARVELING: I fear it, I promise you.
BOTTOM: Masters, you ought to consider with yourself: to bring in – God shield us! – a lion among ladies is a most dreadful thing; for there is not a more fearful wild fowl than your lion living; and we ought to look to't.
SNOUT: Therefore another prologue must tell he is not a lion.
BOTTOM: Nay, you must name his name, and half his face must be seen through the lion's neck, and he himself must speak through, saying thus,

or to the same defect: 'ladies', or 'fair ladies – I would wish you' or 'I would request you' or 'I would entreat you – not to fear, not to tremble. My life for yours: if you think I come hither as a lion, it were pity of my life. No, I am no such thing. I am a man as other men are' – and there indeed let him name his name, and tell them plainly he is Snug the joiner.

QUINCE: Well, it shall be so. But there is too hard things: that is, to bring the moonlight into a chamber – for, you know, Pyramus and Thisbe meet by moonlight.

SNUG: Doth the moon shine that night we play our play?

BOTTOM: A calendar, a calendar! Look in the almanac – find out moonshine, find out moonshine!

QUINCE: Yes, it doth shine that night.

BOTTOM: Why, then may you leave a casement of the Great Chamber window – where we play – open, and the moon may shine in at the casement.

QUINCE: Ay; or else one must come in with a bush of thorns and a lantern, and say he comes to disfigure, or to present, the person of Moonshine. Then there is another thing. We must have a wall in the Great Chamber; for Pyramus and Thisbe, says the story, did talk through the chink of a wall.

SNOUT: You can never bring in a wall. What say you Bottom?

BOTTOM: Some man or other must present Wall; and let him have some plaster, or some loam, or some rough cast about him to signify Wall; and let him hold his fingers thus, and through that cranny shall Pyramus and Thisbe whisper.

QUINCE: If that may be then all is well. Come sit you down every mother's son and rehearse your parts. Pyramus, you begin. When you have spoken your speech, enter into that brake; and so everyone according to his cue.

CHARLES DICKENS

(1812-1870)

Charles Dickens is almost certainly the most famous, widely read, studied and appreciated English novelist: he loved the theatre and through the many dramatisations of his plays had and continues to have a profound influence on it. There is an unsubstantiated suggestion that, as a very young man or even a child, he was an actor in the company of T.D. Davenport at the Portsmouth Theatre and that Davenport's daughter, Jean was the model for the character of the Infant Phenomenon in *Nicholas Nickleby* Certainly we know that Dickens demonstrated his passion for theatre through his many public readings from his novels, his appearances in various productions and the construction of his own small playhouse.

He used his spectacular writing talent to address many of the social injustices of his day. In *Nicholas Nickleby* (1839) he focuses on the plight of children sent to the dubious boarding schools that had proliferated, and where children lived in appalling conditions, simply to line the pockets of the owners.

In order to support himself, his widowed mother and sister, Nicholas takes a post as master at Dotheboys Hall boarding school in Yorkshire. There he befriends the unfortunate Smike, an orphan used as a drudge by Mr and Mrs Squeers, who run the establishment, keeping the boys in constant fear and perpetual hunger. Smike eventually runs away and when Squeers recaptures him he starts to administer a beating, but is stopped by Nicholas who ends up attacking the headmaster. Nicholas then leaves hurriedly but Smike catches up with him and persuades him to let him go with him. At an inn, where they shelter for the night, they are introduced to Mr Vincent Crummles, who runs a travelling theatrical company.

As Paul Schlicke says in his introduction to the Oxford World Classics Series,

"… They provide a fascinating picture of acting practice in the 1839s. Dickens was an inveterate theatre-goer in his young adulthood; not long before he wrote *Nickleby* he aspired to a career on the stage, and amateur theatricals and public readings occupied much of his time in later years. The novel is dedicated to his friend William Charles Macready, the foremost tragedian of the age, and in the Portsmouth scenes Dickens celebrates a subject dear to his heart:

… As characters, the actors offer a haven to Nicholas in a time of troubles, and they constitute a community of positive value.

Nicholas and Smike's adventures commence straight away.

"That'll be a double *encore* if you take care, boys, said Mr Crummles, "You had better get your wind now, and change your clothes."

Having addressed these words to the combatants, he saluted Nicholas, who then observed that the face of Mr Crummles was quite proportionate in size to his body; that he had a very full under-lip, a hoarse voice, as though he were in the habit of shouting very much, and very short black hair, shaved off nearly to the crown of his head – to admit (as he afterwards learnt) of his more easily wearing character wigs of any shape or pattern.

"What did you think of that, Sir?" inquired Mr Crummles.

"Very good, indeed – capital," answered Nicholas.

"You won't see such boys as those very often, I think," said Mr Crummles.

Nicholas assented – observing, that if they were a little better match –

"Match!" cried Mr Crummles.

"I mean if they were a little more of a size," said Nicholas, explaining himself.

"Size!" repeated Mr Crummles; "why, it's the very essence of the combat that there should be a foot or two between them. How are you to get up the sympathies of the audience in a legitimate manner, if there isn't a little man contending against a great one –

"I see," replied Nicholas. "I beg your pardon. That didn't occur to me, I confess."

"It's the main point," said Mr Crummles. "I open at Portsmouth the day after tomorrow. If you are going there look into the theatre, and see how that'll tell."

"Yes, I will."

… Mr Crummles looked from time to time with great interest at Smike, with whom he had appeared considerably struck from the first. He had now fallen asleep, and was nodding in his chair.

"Excuse my saying so," said the manager, "but – what a capital countenance your friend has got!"

"Poor fellow!" said Nicholas, with half a smile, "I wish it were a little more plump and less haggard."

"Plump!" exclaimed the manager, quite horrified, "you'd spoil it for ever."

"Do you think so?"

"Think so, sir!" Why, as he is now," said the manager, striking his knee emphatically; "without a pad upon his body, and hardly a touch of paint upon his face, he'd make such an actor for the starved business as was never seen in this country. Only let him be tolerably well up in the Apothecary in Romeo and Juliet with the slightest possible dab of red on the tip of his nose, and he'd be certain of three rounds the moment he put his head out of the practicable door in the front grooves O.P. … I never saw a young fellow so regularly cut out for that line since I've been in the profession, and I played the heavy children when I was eighteen months old. We'll have a bowl of punch snugly and cosily together by the fire," said Mr Vincent Crummles.

Nicholas was not much disposed to sleep, being in truth too anxious, so after a little demur he accepted the offer.'

But despite the punch and the manager's stories Nicholas was absent and dispirited, with thoughts of his old home and his present condition.

"You are uneasy in your mind," observed Mr Crummles. "What is the matter?"

Nicholas owned that he was under some apprehensions lest he might not succeed in getting something to do which will keep me and my poor fellow-traveller in the common necessaries of life."

"Does no profession occur to you, which a young man of your figure and address could take up easily, and see the world to advantage in?" asked the manager.

"No," said Nicholas, shaking his head.

"Why, then, I'll tell you one," said Mr Crummles, throwing his pipe into the fire, and raising his voice. "The stage."

"The stage!" cried Nicholas, in a voice almost as loud.

"The theatrical profession," said Mr Vincent Crummles. "I am in the theatrical profession myself, my wife is in the theatrical profession, my children are in the theatrical profession. I had a dog that lived and died in it from a puppy; and my chaise-pony goes in Timour the Tartar. I'll bring you out, and your friend too. Say the word. I want a novelty."

"I don't know anything about it," rejoined Nicholas, "I never acted a part in my life, except at school."

"There's genteel comedy in your walk and manner, juvenile tragedy in your eye, and touch-and-go farce in your laugh," said Mr Vincent Crummles. "You do as well as if you had thought of nothing else but the lamps, from your birth downwards."

"You can be useful to us in a hundred ways," said Mr Crummles. "Think what capital bills a man of your education could write for the shop-windows."

"We'll have a new show-piece out directly," said the manager. "Let me see – peculiar resources of this establishment – new and splendid scenery – you must manage to introduce a real pump and two washing-tables."

"Into the piece!" said Nicholas.

"Yes," replied the manager. "I bought 'em cheap, at a sale the other day; and they'll come in admirably. That's the London plan. They look up some dresses, and properties, and have a piece written to fit them. Most of the theatres keep an author on purpose [ ] – a common thing. It'll look very well in the bills in separate lines – Real pump! – Splendid tubs! – Great attraction! You don't happen to be anything of an artist, do you?"

"That is not one of my accomplishments," rejoined Nicholas.

"Ah! Then it can't be helped, said the manager. "If you had been, we might have had a large woodcut of the last scene for the posters, showing the whole depth of the stage, with the pump and tubs in the middle; but however, if you're not, it can't be helped."

"What should I get for all this? Could I live by it?"

"Live by it! Like a prince. With your own salary, and your friend's and your writings, you'd make – ah! You'd make a pound a week!"

"You don't say so."

"I do indeed, and if we had a run of good houses, nearly double the money."

Having agreed they set out at length for Portsmouth, and Mr Crummles pulled up, when they reached the drawbridge.

'They passed a great many bills pasted against the walls and displayed in windows, wherein the names of Mr Vincent Crummles, Mrs Vincent Crummles, Master Crummles, Master P. Crummles, and Miss Crummles, were printed in very large letters, and everything else in very small ones; and turning at length into an entry, in which was a strong smell of orange-peel and lamp-oil, with an under-current of sawdust, groped their way through a dark passage, and, descending a step or two, threaded a little maze of canvass scenes and paint pots, and emerged upon the stage of the Portsmouth Theatre.

"Here we are," said Mr Crummles.

It was not very light, but Nicholas found himself close to the first entrance on the prompter's side, among the bare walls, dusty scenes, mildewed clouds, heavily daubed draperies, and dirty floors. He looked about him; ceiling, pit, boxes, gallery, orchestra, fittings, and decorations of every kind, - all looked coarse, cold, gloomy, and wretched.

"Is this a theatre?" whispered Smike, in amazement; I thought it was a blaze of light and finery."

"Why, so it is," replied Nicholas, hardly less surprised; "but not by day, Smike – not by day."

The manager's voice recalled him from a more careful contemplation of the building, to the opposite side of the proscenium, where, at a small mahogany table with rickety legs and of an oblong shape, sat a stout, portly female, apparently between forty and fifty, in a tarnished silk cloak, with her bonnet dangling by the strings in her hand, and her hair (of which she had a great quantity) braided in a large festoon over each temple.

… "let me introduce Mrs Vincent Crummles."

"I am glad to see you, Sir," said Mrs Vincent Crummles, in a sepulchral voice. "I am very glad to see you, and still more happy to hail you as a promising member of our corps."

"And this," said the lady, crossing to Smike, as tragic actresses cross when they obey a stage direction, "and this is the other. You too, are welcome, Sir."

"He'll do, I think, my dear?" said the manager, taking a pinch of snuff.

"He is admirable," replied the lady. "An acquisition, indeed."

… [T]here bounded onto the stage from some mysterious inlet, a little girl in a dirty white frock with tucks up to the knees, short trousers, sandaled shoes, white spencer, pink gauze bonnet, green veil and curl-papers, who turned a pirouette, cut twice in the air, turned another pirouette, then looking off at the opposite wing shrieked, bounded forward to within six inches of the footlights, and fell into a beautiful attitude of terror, as a shabby gentleman in an old pair of buff slippers came in at one powerful slide, and chattering his teeth, fiercely brandished a walking-stick.

"They are going through the Indian Savage and the Maiden," said Mrs Crummles.

The manager clapped his hands as a signal to proceed, and the Savage, becoming ferocious, made a slide towards the maiden, but the maiden avoided him in six twirls, ad came down at the end of the last one upon the very points of her toes. ... Then the savage and the maiden danced violently together, ...

"Very well indeed," said Mr Cummles; "bravo!"

"Bravo!" cried Nicholas, resolved to make the best of everything. "Beautiful!"

"This, Sir," said Mr Crummles, bringing the maiden forward, "this is the infant phenomenon – Miss Ninetta Crummles."

"Your daughter?" inquired Nicholas.

... "May I ask how old she is?" inquired Nicholas.

"You may, Sir," replied Mr Crummles, looking steadily in his questioner's face ... "She is ten years of age, Sir."

"Not more!"

"Not a day."

"Dear me!" said Nicholas, "it's extraordinary."

It was; for the infant phenomenon, though of short stature, had a comparatively aged countenance, and had moreover been precisely the same age - ... certainly for the last five good years. But she had been kept up late every night, and put upon an unlimited allowance of gin and water from infancy, to prevent her growing tall, and perhaps this system of training had produced in the infant phenomenon these additional phenomena.

"Talent there, Sir, said the savage, nodding towards Miss Crummles.

Nicholas assented.

...

"Ladies and gentlemen," said Mr Vincent Crummles, ... we'll call the Mortal Struggle tomorrow at ten; everybody for the procession. Intrigue, and Ways and Means, you're all up in, so we shall only want one rehearsal. Everybody at ten, if you please."

"Upon my word," said Nicholas, taking the manager aside, "I don't think I can be ready ..."

...

"... my invention is not accustomed to those demands ..."

...

"... Do you understand French?"

"Perfectly well."

"Very good," said the manager, opening the table-drawer, and giving a roll of paper from it to Nicholas. "There, just turn that into

English, and put your name on the title-page. and by that means save all the trouble and expense.

Nicholas worked very hard all day, and did not leave his room until the evening, when he went down to the theatre, whither Smike had repaired before him to go on with another gentleman.

...

Here all the people were so much changed, that he scarcely knew them. False hair, false colour, false calves, false muscles – they had become different beings. Me Lenville was a blooming warrior of most exquisite proportions; Mr Crummles, his large face shaded by a profusion of black hair, a Highland outlaw of most majestic bearing; one of the old gentlemen a gaoler, and the other a venerable patriarch; the comic countryman, a fighting-man of great valour, relieved by a touch of humour; each of the master Crummleses a prince in his own right; and the low-spirited lover, a desponding captive. There was a gorgeous banquet ready spread for the third act, consisting of two pasteboard vases, one plate of biscuits, a black bottle, and a vinegar cruet; and, in short, everything was on a scale of the utmost splendour and preparation.

...

"Been in front tonight?" said Mr Crummles.

"No," replied Nicholas, "not yet. I'm going to see the play."

...

Shortly afterwards the tuning of three fiddles were heard ... being the signal to begin in earnest, set the orchestra playing a variety of popular airs, with involuntary variations.

If Nicholas had been astonished at the alteration for the better which the gentlemen displayed, the transformation of the ladies was still more extraordinary. When, from a snug corner of the manager's box, he beheld Miss Snevellicci in all the glories of white muslin with a golden hem, and Mrs Crummles in all the dignity of the outlaw's wife, and Miss Bravassa in all the sweetness of Miss Snevellicci's confidential friend, and Miss Belwaney in the white silks of a page, ... he could scarcely contain his admiration, which testified itself in great applause ... The plot was most interesting. It belonged to no particular age, people, or country, and was perhaps the more delightful on that account, as nobody's previous information could afford the remotest glimmering of what would ever come of it.

At the end of the piece, the curtain came down amidst general applause.

"What did you think of that?" asked Mr Crummles, when Nicholas went round to the stage again.

"I think it was very capital indeed," replied Nicholas …Miss Snevellicci in particular was uncommonly good"

"Her benefit night, when her friends and patrons bespeak the play," said Mr Crummles. … "Next Monday week. What do you say? You'll have done it, and are sure to be up in the lover's part, long before that time."

"I don't know about 'long before'," replied Nicholas; "but *by* that time I think I can undertake to be ready."

Nicholas worked away at the piece, which was speedily put into rehearsal, and then worked away at his own part, which he studied with great perseverance and acted – as the whole company said – to perfection. And at length the day arrived. The crier was sent round in the morning to proclaim the entertainments with sound of bell in all the thoroughfares; extra bills of three feet long by nine inches wide, were dispersed in all directions, flung down all the areas, thrust under all the knockers, and developed in all the shops; …

At half past five there was a rush of four people to the gallery door; at a quarter before six there were at least a dozen; at six o'clock the kicks were terrific; and when the elder master Crummles opened the door, he was obliged to run behind it for his life. Fifteen shillings were taken by Mrs Grudden in the first ten minutes.

Behind the scenes the same unwonted excitement prevailed. Miss Snevellicci was in such a perspiration that the paint would scarcely stay on her face. Mrs Crummles was so nervous that she could hardly remember her part. Miss Bravassa's ringlets came out of curl with the heat and anxiety; even Mr Crummles himself kept peeping through the hole in the curtain, and running back every now and then to announce that another man had come into the pit.

At last the orchestra left off, and the curtain rose upon the new piece. The first scene, in which there was nobody particular, passed off calmly enough, but when Miss Snevellicci went on in the second, accompanied by the phenomenon as child, what a roar of applause broke out. …

…

But when Nicholas came on for his crack scene with Mrs Crummles, what a clapping of hands there was! When Mrs Crummles (who was his unworthy mother), sneered, and called him 'presumptuous boy', and he defied her, what a tumult of applause came on! When he quarrelled with the other gentleman about the young lady, and producing a case of pistols, said, that if he *was* a gentleman, he would fight him in that drawing-room, till the furniture was sprinkled with the blood of one, if not two people. How boxes, pit, and gallery joined in one most vigorous cheer! When he called his mother names, because she wouldn't give up the young lady's property, and she relenting, caused him to relent likewise, and fall down on one knee and ask her blessing, how the ladies in the audience sobbed! When he was hid behind the curtain in the dark, and the wicked relation poked a sharp sword in every direction, save where his legs were plainly visible, what a thrill of anxious fear ran through the house! His air, his figure, his walk, his look, everything he said or did, was the subject of commendation. There was a round of applause every time he spoke. And when at last, in the pump-and-tub scene, Mrs Grudden lighted the blue fire, and all the unemployed members of the company came in, and tumbled down in various directions - not because that had anything to do with the plot, but in order to finish off with a tableau – the audience … gave vent to such a shout of enthusiasm, as had not been heard in those walls for many and many a day.

In short, the success of both new piece and new actor was complete, and when Miss Snevellicci was called for at the end of the play, Nicholas led her on, and divided the applause."

JOYCE GRENFELL

(1910-1979)

Joyce Grenfell was an English *diseuse*: that is, an actress who specialised in monologues. Many of these, which she wrote herself, reflected her keen observations of childhood. Her mother was the daughter of an American railroad millionaire and her aunt was the well-known Member of Parliament, Nancy Astor, so her own childhood was spent among the rich and famous at Clivedon and in Chelsea. Her first public theatrical appearance was in a programme of her own monologues at the Little Theatre in 1939 and much of this material had been originally devised for the entertainment of family and friends. When war broke out she undertook long and exhausting tours of the Europe, North African the Middle East entertaining troops and after the war she became a familiar face in films and television. Perhaps her most memorable roles were as the games teacher, Miss Gossage in *The Happiest Days of your Life* and as Ruby Gates in the 'St. Trinian's' films

Her family had always been immersed in theatre: in her autobiography *Joyce Grenfell Requests the Pleasure* (London: Macmillan, 1976).
–she wrote of her grandparents:]

"The Wilton Phippses went regularly to 'the play', and they always had a box.

They went to see Henry Arthur Jones's play *The Dancing Girl* at the Theatre Royal, Haymarket, five times. On 4 April my grandmother went with four friends to the Criterion Theatre to see *The School for Scandal* and wrote that they were 'much amused' at the supper party afterwards given by Charles Wyndham in his room, overlooking Piccadilly Circus, 'furnished like a cabin in a yacht'.

My parents had many theatrical friends and I had been stage-struck ever since my first visit to the theatre. (It was a revue at the Hippodrome called *A Box of Tricks*, and I fell in love with the chorus which I thought were all little girls because they did a skipping-rope number and wore ankle-socks.)

The only real talent I had was wholly instinctive: I could invent characters and pretend I was someone else. As soon as I could talk I playacted with my mother, making up conversations about our imaginary children. We sat side by side on the drawing-room sofa and invented together. At first I imitated talk I had heard from her and Lucy. Then I ranged further and became other kinds of talkers with other voices. One invention was an old ma, but most of my characters were mothers with children and I imagined them in shops, by the sea, having meals. Apparently my fantasies took me on long journeys, and my ma, feeding me questions, was captivated.

When I was eight and quite portly she came into the bathroom and found me standing at attention in the water, saluting. I had arranged my bath-cap into a peak. … She asked me with just enough interest in her voice to encourage an answer: "What are you doing?" "I'm "I'm Princess Mary reviewing the troops on a yacht."

In most things I was not as self-assured as I appeared to be. "Being funny", making up characters, came easily, but it wasn't until I went on the stage that I learned to discipline what I invented; and by then I had some concentration and worked with purpose and some self-criticism. At school I went on observing and reproducing what I observed, and when my friends laughed it egged me on to do more. … For three years until I went away to boarding school in late 1924 Dorothy Gillespie, Carley Robinson and I made up a trio. … We were all movie- and stage-mad. …Often on Saturdays we … dressed up in our mothers' clothes and acted to music. This meant long sessions experimenting with our hair and our mothers' make-up (face powder, pale rouge, and lip-salve with a hint of pink in it). Then we acted. That is to say we took up postures and emoted. We were enclosed in our own private dreams and took very little notice of each other. Music was used to stir us and create a mood, and when I tell you the two most regularly employed records were *Jewels of the Madonna* by Wolf-Ferrari and selections from *Madame Butterfly* you will see that we were not very like little girls of today.

Dorothy's house had an L-shaped drawing-room and we acted in the L bit of it. We used a brocade-covered pouffe as a stage prop, and I stood on it pretending I was about to be swept away into the sea. Now and then we drew each other's attention. "Look! – I'm being passionate." We heaved our faintly indicated bosoms, just beginning to show under our jerseys, and we rolled our eyes. We showed fear as we had seen Alice Terry do it in *Scaramouche,* putting the back of our right hand, fingers stiffly splayed, in front of our open mouths, and leaned against the wall, facing invisible horrors. We did stage faints with great thuds and resulting bruises; we registered tragedy and pain; tried to make ourselves produce real tears by thinking of something sad, but we never, never played happiness. Our heroines in the movies went through hell and, being happy and secure, we enjoyed pretending to suffer as they did. Because of my height I was usually the "villain". At Doro's we had no men's clothes but I drew a moustache with burnt cork and spoke low in what I believed to be a suave manner. I would have preferred to play the feminine lead.

I became aware that I was being watched and that the watchers were amused. I did not have to open my eyes to see this; I felt it and I liked the feeling. I have never lost this liking.

When I was twelve I wished I was an actress. … I did not ache to play Rosalind or in *Bluebell in Fairyland*. I didn't think about words or rehearsals – indeed I didn't want to act. I dreamed … that I was an actress. I was in love with the idea of actresses because my family had friends who worked in the theatre and their pictures were in the papers. They seemed more interesting than other people and far more glamorous.

At that stage I was in love with both Noel Coward and Ivor Novello at the same time … Both came to the house and, because they were fond of my mother, paid special attention to me. Noel had been brought to luncheon by Mrs Patrick Campbell on my tenth birthday … (All I remember about Mrs Pat on this occasion were her big black velvet picture-hat, piercing black eyes and her searching question to me, spoken in a deep theatrical voice: "Are you *happy*?" I stored this up and used it years later I invented an earnest soul-searcher I called Fern

Brixton.) Ivor Novello sent my mother a bunch of Parma violets and I told a school friend he had sent them to me. She was amazed, but impressed.

I persuaded my parents that I was serious about giving into the theatre. I think I meant it, but I have no recollection of imagining what I wanted to do once I got there. The only training I ever had was the weekly elocution lesson with Mrs Alvey at my school, Clear View, in South Norwood on a hill near the Crystal Palace.

We did vocal exercises together with Vivien Alderson. Deep breath; then, starting on a low note, she began: "Adjels and bidisters of Grace defend us." She moved up a tone. "Adjels and bidisters of Grace defend us," and so on up the scale, teaching us to articulate clearly on the slowly released breath. Mrs Alvey, who didn't wear corset, invited her pupils to feel the iron discipline of her stomach-muscles by pressing as hard as they could on the beige inserted panel of her long plum-brown princess-line dress. She relied on Shakespeare to develop our vocal techniques. "The quality of bercy is not strain'd", she boomed, and I boomed after her. I was allowed to choose my own recitations and over-acted in Jean Ingelow's *High Tide on the Coast of Lincolnshire*. I felt worldly and bitter in *The Forsaken Merman*. These recitations were rendered with intensity and not one glimmer of humour.

I had played my first part on any as a tinsel fairy in an improvised version of *Hansel and Gretel*, in Aunt Nancy's drawing-room at Cliveden in the First World War, before an audience of wounded solders. I was five. The role of the fairy was demanding. I had to hold a wand with a star on it in one hand and a single leaf in the other. The part called for me to trip on lightly, spot the unfortunate children sleeping on the ground and drop my leaf as a means of disguising their presence from the wicked villains who were out to get them. Not only was this a first time on any stage, it was also a first time of wearing proper, long, grown-up white stockings – joy, oh joy, the feel of them, buttoned on to what was inaccurately known as a liberty bodice by tapes sewn to their tops. Tape doesn't yield, so after I had knelt to deliver my leaf and risen jerkily to a standing position there were sagging knees to the white stockings and quite a lot of wrinkling at the ankles. It seems I was in no hurry to get off the stage and stood there smiling in my tinselly sparkle and wobbly wings while my stockings crept down my legs.

...

When I was eight I was miscast as a starving Burgher of Calais in a school play at Pavilion Road.

...

At my next, much grander school, Francis Holland, Graham Street ... there was a full-scale production of *As You Like It*. The Upper School played the leading parts but representatives of the lower orders had their roles and mine was a truncated version of the First Lord. ... Cut down to one speech ... it was practically invisible.

...

At my final and happiest school, Clear View, I was more at home in a cockney one-acter called *The 'At*. By this time I was the tallest girl in the school and except for the part of Miss Pole in *Cranford* I was always cast as a man. So boring.

...

When it was decided that I should have a try at acting, my father talked to an old friend from the Lutyens office days, Nicholas Hannen, then a successful actor. He advised me to try and get into the Royal Academy of Dramatic Art where another contemporary of my father's was the Principal. Kenneth Barnes asked me to come and see him in his office and I did a bit of *As You Like It*, as taught me by Mrs Alvey. Somehow I got into RADA and I began in the autumn term of 1927. ...

I lasted one term at the Academy and played one tiny part in a French play. ... That is all I remember of my days at RADA except that Celia Johnson was in the play too. ... Unlike me, and most of the others, she didn't want to be thought to be an actress, she wanted to act. She was very short-sighted and wore steel-rimmed glasses. Even in those early days everything she did showed talent and style. I looked on her with awe and admiration and I still do.

…

Apart from school performances I had no experience in amateur entertainment until around 1930 a group of us got up a fund-raising concert at Tunbridge Wells. Someone suggested we should call ourselves The Bright Spots and no one had the courage to say no. … [T]here is an unkind pleasure in watching bad amateurs, so perhaps the charity supporters at the Pump Room that night had some fun.

…

For The Bright Spots I designed and hand-painted the girls' costumes – white Roman furnishing satin sheets with stiff net Pierrot frills at the neck and around the hem. Bunches of bright flowers appeared all over the place painted in coloured waterproof inks, and we each had a different coloured hair-ribbon and sash.

*   *   *

I think I lost interest in acting in plays because I found it too restrictive. The lines were set and there was no room for spontaneous invention. In a play you had to wait to be spoken to before you could speak. This was not for me.

…

Gerard du Maurier was a real star at that time, and my cup was full when he took me down to supper and told me that I looked like his father's drawings. … In 1945 I wrote a song with Richard Addinsell about a young du Maurier woman and sang it in Noel Coward's peace-time revue *Sigh No More*.

*   *   *

At a party Herbert Farjeon persuaded Joyce to give a re-run of her "Women's Institute Lecture".

"May I ask who wrote that piece you just did?"

No one wrote it", I . "It was mostly a *real* talk to our Women's Institute meeting in the country, and I embroidered on it."

"Do you think you could write it down? I'd like to use it in my new revue.

…

At first I didn't seriously entertain this crazy idea ... but Bertie wrote and asked me to think again about his offer. He seemed convinced I'd succeed on the stage and said he thought I should try it and see. It seemed foolish not to take the risk but ... I didn't particularly want to go on the stage.

This oddly enough was true. I was contented with the quiet life in the country ... and here was an invitation, unexpected and unsought, decidedly flattering but disruptive ...

[To her mother she wrote:]

I forgot to tell you that Mr Farjeon actually wanted me to come into the revue but I don't think I would be good on a stage – I may do all right in a small room but the stage is quite different. Anyway he wrote to me and said that if I ever did want to I must let him know at once, whether tomorrow or in five years' time! Nice that.

…

Not for a moment, even then, did I think of the theatre as a career. Writing was what I wanted to do and if I went into the revue it would be a once-only experience, certainly an adventure.

…

My father thought I might as well have a try – why not? And my husband, who is a very wise man and realised he would have to go on living with me whatever I decided, said: "You had better do it because you'll always think you *could* have done it if you don't. [However], with these encouragements I told Bertie I would come into his new show.

…

Our compere was Ronnie Walters, six foot three with flaming red hair. … [H]e announced me with tremendous zest.

"And *now* … *direct* form the Women's Institute … Miss …Joyce … GRENFELL."

It was the sort of introduction that leads the audience to expect an entrance, naked, on an elephant. Instead it got me in my grey chiffon and little pinky red jacket. They applauded warmly and I later discovered the place was full of friends, supporters of the good cause, who had come for that reason and for the remembered joys of Bertie's previous revue. They were, I think, surprised to see me one stage and clapped to encourage me.

But then something happened. I began, as all real Women's Institute lecturers begin:

""Madam President – Fellow Institute Members – good evening."

I spoke in the dainty way of the original speaker and I suppose the audience recognised the authenticity of what I said and how I said it. We were off. I said alone. They laughed. I said another. They laughed. It was a sort of game, with me holding back the next line till the last moment and then letting them have it. An audience, a responsive audience, was what I had missed in all those dull rehearsals. Now the thing worked, now I could experiment with it, certain of the way I wanted it to go. I felt as if I were riding a marvellous great white flying horse in perfect rhythm, with perfect control …

I have never again had quite such an astonishing and thrilling experience with an audience. It was a first time so good that it gave me confidence, enough to know that such a relationship between performer and audience was possible. I walked off to prolonged applause.

Joyce was to go on to become one of our best-loved performers, despite the fact that [extract:] "It was not until I was already on stage, performing my own monologues, that I realised the genre was not familiar to everyone."

She went a long way towards remedying this, becoming one of our best-loved entertainers, but always insisting that it was the audience who must supply the imagination.

GRAHAM GREENE

(1904-1991)

Graham Greene was one of the great literary figures of the twentieth century and is probably best known today through his novels *Brighton Rock, The Power and the Glory, The Heart of the Matter* and *The End of the Affair.* Some of his novels, such as *The Confidential Agent, The Third Man, The Quiet American* and *Our Man in Havana* reveal a profound knowledge of and fascination with international espionage and under-cover working and several have been made into memorable films. What is often overlooked is that Greene was also a substantial playwright and, of his eight published plays, *The Living Room, The Potting Shed* and *The Return of A.J.Raffles* were almost certainly the most successful.

Story telling in some dramatic form was an essential part of Greene's upbringing in a family of six children with highly intelligent and cultivated parents. These early years are beautifully documented in Norman Sherry's impressive biography, *The Life of Graham Greene Vol. One 1904-1939.* Family life revolved around the fact that Greene's father was second master (and eventually headmaster) at Berkhamsted School in Hertfordshire and that other affluent branches of the Greene family lived nearby. When the young Graham was seven years old he took part in a competition run by the school which consisted of responding to a questionnaire. He listed 'Going up to London' as his 'Greatest idea of Happiness' and Sir Walter Scott's *The Talisman* as 'The Author and book he liked Best'.

It would appear that the main reason for the Greene children being taken to London was the annual Christmas visit to see the play *Peter Pan*. His biographer tells us:

Once a year, at Christmas, the children were taken to see *Peter Pan* at the Duke of York's Theatre. Graham loved it, his favourite scene being when Peter Pan fought alone against the pirates with his sword, and second to that was the moment of enjoyable horror when the green-lit face of Captain Hook appeared at a service hatch and put poison into Peter's glass. Although the dying fairy, tinker Bell, touched him, he would never call out with the audience that he believed in fairies in order to save her as he had a deeply felt need to be honest: "It would have been dishonest, for I had never believed in fairies, except for the period of the play".

This, of course, is precisely what is meant by the 'suspension of disbelief' during the performance of a play and shows a remarkable ability to recognise this. Looking back on Christmas at home Greene recalled that it was a time of charades and family amateur theatricals.

His sister, Elizabeth, remembered the popularity of Saki's *The Unrest Cure* and even when he was twenty two, Graham himself reported that "I've had to invent an impromptu play for Raymond and Charlotte and Hugh and Elizabeth and me to act on Christmas night, a sort of acrobatic charade. It's horribly gruesome

Drama and theatre remained an essential ingredient throughout Greene's life and, indeed, may well have formed a type of therapy. The once very literate and imaginative child with his own secret spaces and solitary activities was bullied at boarding school and eventually suffered a breakdown. However, even before undergoing psychoanalysis he returned to school and acted in a play:

The Berkhamstedian reports that 'on the evening of 4th June 1921, the St. John's Dramatic Society presented Lord Dunsany's play *The Lost Silk Hat*, with H.G. (Graham) Greene playing the part of the poet.

During his subsequent psychiatric treatment by the brilliant Kenneth Richmond Greene took up residence in London where he was visited by cousins and aunts: one of his chief pleasures was visiting the Theatre:

…when his cousin Ave came they went to see Eugene O'Neill's *Anna Christie*, and also visited the London Assizes together: 'It was Graham's idea to go to the Old Bailey because we didn't have enough money to go to the theatre often. Graham would ask the Bobby on duty in the forecourt which were the most exciting cases on and we'd go and spend the whole afternoon there'.

In October, he and his aunt bought tickets for Gilbert and Sullivan's *The Gondoliers* ('our sets were excellent…. A large proportion of evening dresses….Lytton and Sheffield were wonderful'), and they went to see the play *Christopher Sly*: 'the show was the best I've ever seen. Matheson Lang acted beautifully. Florence Saunders was an extremely pretty girl''Arthur Whitby awfully good as a strolling player…the end was wonderful. The dead body of Christopher Sly lying in the dark cellar, and slowly the light of the lantern approaching and the voices of the guards, coming nearer, singing a drinking catch, coming to let free Sly, to let him return to his tavern and bottle'.

Greene's biographer, Norman Sherry, drawing on primary sources, provides a fascinating account of Greene's subsequent theatrical activities in the light of his early enthusiasm:
He points out that in Greene's book *Ways of Escape* (1980) the writer discusses his novels *Stanboul Train* and *A Gun for Sale*, and says :

' I can detect in both books the influence of my early passion for play-writing which has never quite died'. Sherry continues:
And certainly his interest in the theatre, which started at school, increased at University where he went through the whole gamut of theatrical experience as actor, playwright and entrepreneur. He wrote to his mother during his first month at University: 'A new dramatic society has just been formed at Balliol for the production of plays by undergraduates…I just missed getting mine taken.
Six months later there was a Balliol drama competition, Graham submitted a second play (we do not have the title of either) and one of the judges, possibly Harley Granville Barker, found it 'marred by sentimentality', though stressing not 'banal sentimentality'. He found that it was competent within it own limits, and had a certain charm. He added: 'If, as I venture to suppose, you are as yet fortunately young, it is exactly as it should be for your future development. I feel fairly sure that…we shall hear of you again.'
At Oxford he tried to form his own drama company. He wrote to his mother: 'the first week of next vacation we are going for a tramp, acting plays in villages.' Typical of his energy is the extraordinary speed with which he put this idea into operation. His letter continues: 'Raymond

may be coming. Otherwise it consists of self, Fergusson (Balliol), Gust, Cockburn, York-Lodge (Keble). I got going fairly quickly, as I formed the idea at 11.15 Tuesday morning, and had got the company together by tea time; and had decided on one play. We are doing three one –acters, of which one is the *Monkey's Paw* (by W.W. Jacobs). Guest is taking any properties we need in his side car.' Financially alert, he asks: 'P.S. To get off the Entertainment Tax, must all takings go to charity? Or only profits?' Though that particular venture fell through, another was started, a purely Balliol affair with more ambitious plays. They decided on *Macbeth* with Graham taking the part of Banquo, and an English doctor and 'Wilde's *The Importance of Being Earnest* which I am stage managing, and acting as a young bounder'.

Joseph Macleod recalls that Greene acted in a play of his at Oxford in 1924. 'My play, *The Fog Spider,* was a psychological –symbolical-something-or- other protest against suburban family life. I played the Father, Peter Quennell my Wife…and Graham my son. The action really took place inside the son's neurotic brain, and Graham did try to establish some atmosphere of terror with eyes staring, hands clutching and extending and back bent. But we all lacked experience. What was meant as dead tragic was found by the audience killingly comic. It was a disaster.'

HAROLD PINTER

(1930-2009)

For many theatre enthusiasts and critics Harold Pinter was the greatest English playwright of the second half of the twentieth century. His tense, disturbing and verbally intriguing plays seem to encapsulate the sense of menace and problematic communications that lurk beneath the surface of modern life. Pinter entered the theatre as an actor before establishing himself as a playwright and screen writer and his first-hand experience clearly helped to shape his unerring grasp of the theatrical moment. From seeing his early one-act play *The Room* premiered at the University of Bristol and his first full-length play, *The Birthday Party* performed to a virtually empty London theatre, Pinter progressed to the point where his plays were widely produced and studied and each new play greeted as a major theatrical event.

The distinguished theatre critic, Michael Billington, provides brief but significant glimpses of the early events and influences that helped to shape Harold Pinter's writing in his book *The Life and Work of Harold Pinter* (1996). Pinter was born in North East London and grew up during the Second World War. His childhood included periods of evacuation but his most vivid memories appear to have been those of his East End Jewish family and relations with their differing degrees of devoutness and scepticism. Harold was an only child and, like so many children, he established a world of imaginary friends.

As if in preparation for the inner landscapes that he would create for his dramatic characters, he peopled the theatre of his mind with fictional friends. Billington reports Pinter as saying:

"I don't know how it would have changed my life if I'd had brothers and sisters, but I can say one thing, I created a small body of imaginary friends in the back garden when I was about eight or nine. We had a lilac tree with an arch and beyond that arch was an untended piece of garden. I made that my home where I met these invisible friends who certainly weren't brothers and sisters but were definitely all boys. I had this total fantasy life in which we talked aloud and held conversations beyond the lilac tree. There was also – still is apparently – a laundry at the back of the garden so I was having this fantasy life with the laundry roaring away."

For many young people, the world of theatre and literature is revealed through the skill and enthusiasm of dedicated and inspirational teachers: Pinter's early years illustrate this fact and emphasise the importance of an education free from undue regulation and restraints that enables teachers to impart knowledge and passion for a subject:
At Hackney Downs Grammar School Pinter was fortunate because:
"He encountered one of those enlightened English teachers who opens up new horizons, made a number of lifelong friends and explored his young life, it was in his late teens; and if his work is full of the echoes and memories of some lost paradise, then the Grammar School years are his own personal touchstone.

The school itself has had an extraordinary history. It was founded in the 1870s by the Grocers' Company in exact imitation of a Prussian prototype. It was handed over to the then London County Council early in the century and, in the 1940s, by virtue of Hackney demographics, had an over 50 per cent Jewish intake and a high regard for learning. In its time it has produced two life peers, two university vice-chancellors and two famous actor-playwrights in Pinter and Steven Berkoff. Sadly, it was closed by the Secretary of State for Education and Employment in 1995 because of falling standards, but in Pinter's day it encouraged – at least among the staff – an eccentric individualism. The most influential figure on Pinter was an English teacher called Joe Brearley: a tall Yorkshireman who suffered from malaria, had been torpedoed at sea in the war and who was wont to march down corridors crying at the top of his voice, "Othello's occupation's gone." In fact, Brearley seemed to have found his *metier* in Hackney and passed on his passion for English poetry and drama to Pinter and other pupils. For Pinter, Brearley became counsellor, intellectual mentor and lifelong friend. "We embarked," Pinter remembers, on a series of long walks, which continued for years, starting from Hackney Downs, up to Springfield Park, along the River Lea, back up Lea Bridge Road, past Clapton Pond, through Mare Street to Bethnal Green." On their walks they would declaim passages from Webster into the wind or at passing trolley-buses. Fifty years later, when receiving the David Cohen British Literature Prize, Pinter would recall: "That language made me dizzy. Joe Brearley fired my imagination. I can never forget him." .

Billington goes on to provide a rich insight into Pinter's early experience of theatre, both as an audience member and actor. His later mastery of the use of the 'pause' and 'silence' may well have owed something to the young Pinter's having seen the powerful and distinctive performances of actors in an older tradition typified by Donald Wolfit but one also senses that seeing plays in performance took the young Pinter to new levels of emotional development:…..

"It was at this time that Pinter, already besotted by poetry and fiction, woke up to the power of drama. Joe Brearley – who was an adopted paternal member of the gang – dragged them off to see Donald Wolfit playing Shakespeare at the People's Palace in the East End and at the Bedford, Camden Town. In 1947 he also took them up West to see Michael Bethall's production of *The White Devil* at the Duchess starring Margaret Rawlings and Robert Helpmann. "it made ordinary life," says Woolf, "seem terribly boring. This was life to the power of twenty-three. It had a terrific impact on Harold and the rest of us." Webster's poetry – tangy and bitter, full of warning and irrepressibly sombre" in the words of Kenneth Tynan writing about that same production – left its dark imprint on Pinter's imagination and on much of his early verse. Not only did he stroll through Hackney declaiming Webster with Brearley; even today I've heard him round off a supper party by quoting from memory Bosola's dirge in *The Duchess of Malfi*, relishing the lines "Their life a general mist of error, Their death a hideous storm of terror" and playfully asking guests to identify the source. And when Andy in *Moonlight* declares "The past is a mist" you can still hear the influence of Webster's chill compression on Pinter's language and thought.".

The experience of seeing live theatre was later reinforced by Pinter's first serious attempt at acting Shakespeare.

"Pinter's theatregoing was accompanied by a discovery of the joy of acting. One day in 1947 Brearley announced to the class that he would do a production of *Macbeth*, adding somewhat peremptorily, "And you, Pinter, will play Macbeth." And so he did, wearing the khaki uniform of a modern British soldier. "I was so pleased with this uniform," says Pinter, "that I wore it on the 38 bus to go home to tea after the dress-rehearsal. Old ladies smiled at me. The bus conductor looked at me and said, 'Well, I don't know what to charge you.'" Even more surprising than Pinter's infatuation with uniform is that he earned his first recognition in print from Alsn Dent, whom Brearley persuaded to come along and review the production in the *New Chronicle*. "All in all", wrote Dent, it was a clearly spoken, though dimly lit, production and Master Harold Pinter made a more eloquent, more obviously nerve-racked Macbeth than one or two professional grown-ups I have seen in the part of late years." Heady praise for any boy-actor. That it meant a lot to Pinter was proved when he and Dent met in a TV studio in the mid-1960s during the recording of an arts programme. Dent was somewhat embarrassed because he'd been noticeably cool about Pinter's early plays. According to the nervous critic, Pinter assured him, "Don't you worry about that, Mr Dent. You gave me the most treasured notice I ever had as an actor and I still keep it at home tucked away in my Shakespeare."

MARGARET RUTHERFORD

(1892-1972)

Margaret Rutherford became one of Britain's best-loved actresses. Her many chins and air of sublime eccentricity made her an unforgettable character in any production. She had a painful childhood because the family secret was that her father had murdered his own father and had spent much of his life in a lunatic asylum. It was many years before Margaret, who lived with Auntie Bessie, discovered he was still living. As a lonely, only child, always known as 'Peggy' she was joined at holiday times by her cousin, Graham Nicholson, and, together, they made up their own plays. At the age of thirty three Margaret Rutherford wrote 'I began my stage career late in life and the beginning was not easy. If you want to be an actor or an actress passionately enough, you will be-but it is up to you to persevere, despite all obstacles'.

Her adopted daughter, Dawn Langley Simmons, wrote a biography of Margaret: *Margaret Rutherford: A Blithe Spirit* (1983) in which she tells of early family theatrical enterprises and how these led to a developing career in the profession:

As was the fashion in those times of self-entertainment, family theatricals, especially melodrama, were enacted. (Aunt Bessie's favourite was *Maria Martin* or *Murder in the Red Barn*). On such game-playing occasions, Margaret and Graham, who were very compatible 'had to endure our cousin Muriel, who was so anti-theatre that I had to write a part for her where she was confined to a dark, dreary cupboard for most of the performance.

At the age of eight, Margaret was to have played the Bad Fairy in the Nicholson's annual Christmas play; when Graham conveniently 'went down with an ear infection and the mumps,' she obligingly took over his Fairy Prince role as well.

She never forgot that first all-important entrance, as one of the adults laboured behind the scenes to produce necessary claps of thunder from a rolling pin and a battered tin tray! A professional actress in the friendly audience gave her her first good notice, as the Bad Fairy. 'The child has great histrionic power,' she announced to a proud Aunt Bessie. 'One has to be really good to be bad.'

That night, Margaret Rutherford went to bed filled with dreams of growing up to be a great actress.

Then Auntie Bessie decided to make what Margaret called 'The Supreme Sacrifice.' Deciding that it was time that her beloved child 'be prepared for the real world…for she simply cannot live in her own fairyland for ever.' Aunt Bessie enrolled her at Raven's Croft School in Upper Warlingham, Surrey. When Margaret went to Raven's Croft, she was fourteen years old; the year was 1906.

Raven's Croft was a reputable school for girls, founded by two exceptional sisters, Margaret and Isabelle Mullins. When Isabelle asked Margaret what she would like to be when she grew up, she received the matter-of-fact reply: 'As I am already a lady, I want nothing better that to be a professional actress.' The little gold pince-nez spectacles dropped off Miss Isabelle's nose. She was shocked at such a revelation. 'I suspect,' said Margaret,' that the poor dear lady had visions of Lily Langtry the actress and her unhealthy liaison with King Edward the Seventh.'

Next day Margaret was confronted by both head-mistresses, who proclaimed it their joint opinion that 'young ladies did not become actresses, professional or otherwise.' Instead, as her piano playing showed much promise, they decided that for the next six years Margaret Rutherford should study for the associate examination of the Royal Academy of Music, which, in due course, she would pass with honours Years later, after the school had moved further along the coast to Eastbourne, her name 'P. Rutherford' remained painted on one of the prefect boards that hung in the school's assembly hall.

One year while at Seaford, Margaret played Prospero in *The Tempest*, which was performed by the 'big girls'

It would appear that her teachers no longer thought that there was a danger of her following her ambition to become an actress. This, however, was not the case and, although she left school in 1911 and became a familiar sight in the streets of Wimbledon riding her bicycle and swinging her leather music case from the handlebars as she visited her piano students, she still sought ways of fulfilling her

dream. She enrolled as a student of a famous elocution teacher, Acton Bond and, as a result gained a certificate of proficiency in the subject, even though this involved practising her vowel sounds as she rode her cycle

During the First World War she not only acted in the local dramatic society, accepting any role, 'however humble' but she entertained soldiers on leave and in hospital with poetry recitations

Her biographer tells of her introduction to the famous Old Vic Theatre by a somewhat circuitous route:

Dorothy Whatmore, Margaret's former schoolmate, had written her a letter of introduction to John Drinkwater, poet and dramatist. Drinkwater in turn referred her to Robert Atkins, a former head of the Old Vic School. Atkins thought she should see Andrew Leigh, who had succeeded him in that formidable position.

As a result, the would- be actress received a letter saying that she had been granted an audition with Lilian Baylis, then affectionately (or otherwise) known as the Queen Of the Old Vic. Such stage and screen greats as John Gielgud, Laurence Olivier, Edith Evans, and Ralph Richardson were all to owe Miss Baylis a debt for their early training. Margaret was elated. Wearing her best green dress (green was her favourite colour) and a pair of fashionable new Gloria Swanson pointed shoes that looked somewhat out of place on her rather large, broad feet, she jumped on the bus for Waterloo. At long last, she hoped, her chance had come.

Miss Baylis was a no-nonsense lady and, to Margaret that day, quite a frightening one. With thick-lensed glasses, mousey hair, and what Margaret described as a 'one-sided smile' she was flanked on either side by a snappy terrier,

Margaret Rutherford's audition was a near disaster. 'My new shoes let out miaowing squeaks every time I walked, even making the dog's bark.' At the end of the audition the Queen of the Old Vic pronounced, in her most gloomy, godlike voice: 'Dear girl, I think production might be a safer line than acting'.

Although we shall never know what changed her mind, Lilian Baylis contacted Margaret a few days later to inform her that she had been accepted as a 'trainee actress' for the September 1925-May 1926 season.

She lived in much awe of Miss Baylis during her days a the Old Vic School. Lilian Baylis liked to sit in her office, feet up on a chair, listening to classical music on her crystal radio set; only the dogs were allowed to disturb her.

Margaret discovered the Old Vic to be a just but hard school. The students were obliged to take any role given them; on 21st December, she received what she called 'a wonderful Christmas gift….my first speaking role'. She played the Fairy with the long nose in *Harlequin Jack Horner and the Enchanted Pie.* She apparently wore her papier-mache snout with distinction. The second offering of the evening was a nativity play, *The Child of Flanders* by Cicely Hamilton, with Edith Evans playing a mute Angel Gabriel. Gabriel's lines were spoken offstage by Margaret, who was obliged to remove her extra nose as she dashed to the rear. An outspoken critic wrote 'Edith Evans' elocution has greatly improved'.

In this way, Margaret had almost certainly provided some children with *their* first experience of live theatre! Almost unconsciously, her bibliographer provides some fascinating insights into Lilian Baylis's autocratic rule and the performance style of the Old Vic in our next extract, and also highlights the vital importance of the amateur theatre for which Britain is almost unique,

After winning a student competition, Margaret played Lady Capulet to Edith Evans' Nurse in *Romeo and Juliet.* Esmond Knight, Frank Vosper and Baliol Holloway were in the same cast; all five were destined for successful careers in the theatre. In (Shaw's) *Antony and Cleopatra,* Margaret had one line to recite over Caesar's bier. 'I enunciated each word so that a deaf man in the upper circle could hear it. I was so grateful to be doing at last what I loved most,' she said. But after giving her eleven roles to play in nine months, Miss Baylis casually called Margaret into the office, turned of the crystal radio, and told the dogs to be quiet. Then the Queen of the Old Vic with regal finality announced that she was sorry but there would be no room for Margaret in the next season. 'Somehow you just do not fit in!'

Instead of dwelling on the Old Vic's rejection, she quickly joined the Wimbledon Amateur Theatrical Society where she first displayed that natural gift she had for bringing laughter to her audience. This was an army dishwashing scene, where she managed to break more cups than she wiped

'It was then,' she said, 'that I felt the joy it gave me in being able to make people laugh and forget themselves…..Never look down on the humble art of washing up. Who knows but in every shining cup and saucer will be reflected a character from your next play.'

She also found a stage godmother in Ethel Royale, who had successfully appeared opposite Cedric Hardwicke in *The Farmer's Wife.* As a special favour, Margaret's uncle, Guy Nicholson, had asked Miss Royale, a personal friend, to see his niece in the Wimbledon production of *Hay Fever* and tell him truthfully if his niece should continue in her efforts to be an actress. Margaret was playing the comic maid and knew in advance that Ethel Royale would be in the audience. 'I can truthfully say that I did not feel so nervous on my wedding day.'

Afterwards Miss Royale assured Uncle Guy that 'you Peggy is lovable and will make people laugh, both rare qualities in the theatre.

However, despite her great and continuing success in comedy, including a memorable Miss Prism in Gielgud's production of *The Importance of Being Ernest* and her best- remembered role as Madam Arcati in *Blithe Spirit*, Margaret longed to be thought of as a serious actress. Robert Morley, a life-long friend, had said: 'Margaret can root out a laugh like a truffle hound!' but she enjoyed seasons in repertory companies which gave her the experience of plays by Ibsen, Pinero, Maughan and Coward. At Croydon she had the opportunity to appear with Donald Wolfit in Ibsen's *The Master Builder* and this prompted the playwright Ronald Harwood, to say some years later 'Alas, I never met Dame Margaret, whom I greatly admired. I do, however, remember Sir Donald Wolfit saying that she was the best Mrs Solness he ever played with; he also said that she had the qualities of a great tragic actress and he did not use the word 'great' lightly'.

Film roles included the Headmistress in *The Happiest Days of Your Life*, Nurse Carey in *Miranda* ,Professor Hatton-Jones in *Passport to Pimlico,* a reprise of Madam Arcati in *Blithe Spirit* and an appearance with Orson Welles in *Chimes at Midnight.* Indeed, at one point she was the highest paid British film artist, but alongside that,

simple poetry performances were always part of her life and she played in theatres, churches, prisons and asylums as well as taking part in E.N.S.A. tours with Ivor Novello and music and poetry tours with Malcolm Troup.

Thinking back over her career, Dame Margaret, as she became said:
But there is more latitude in eccentrics. They are always honest, and have their own quality of madness. In the final assessment, I think they will be the saints'.

We shall; never know if she was still thinking about her father.

MARK WOOLGAR

(b.1941)

Mark's initiation into the world of Theatre is summarised in his memories below. After a brief spell as a teacher, introducing Drama to a new secondary school, he won a trainee Theatre director's position with the Bristol Old Vic Company, though he had only directed adults once (amateurs in Gilbert and Sullivan's *Iolanthe*). Along the way in a career which has taken him as an actor from Los Angeles to Aberdeen, and as a director from Sophocles to Godber, he has doubled the attendance figures of an English regional theatre, headed various vocational Acting courses, devised a Foundation Degree in Acting, adapted novels for the stage, toured his own Oscar Wilde show widely, overseen new professional performing qualifications and remained a voracious attender at all kinds of 'shows'.

Of his first memory of theatre he writes:

> 'Yum, yum,yum, I love my tum
> And my tum tum loves me too'

Faintly down the years from the 1940s linger these chorus lines from the 'songsheet' of a York Theatre Royal pantomime. As also does the embarrassment of the competitive singing then decreed by the comic in charge of the songsheet when, with house lights up, the 'paupers up there' were encouraged to sing louder than 'you rich lot down here' – and I knew I was only in the 'rich' section because I was the guest of a family better off than my own. Class loomed larger then . Never mind – I learned quickly and the next year knew this was all really only a 'vamp till ready' and soon the frontcloth would rise (yet again !) and there would be the grand staircase and the entire cast floating down in glittery new costumes for the Curtain Call and the breathlessness of the leader of that 'songsheet' routine as he shot down the stairs would betray the speed of his costume change. And this grand finale would make up for the slight disillusion caused by that frontcloth. 'Twenty spectacular scenes' promised the posters but about half of them were that same old frontcloth and no amount of chicanery in the programme ('ANOTHER part of the woods' indeed !) could wipe out the slight feeling of fraudulence. But pantomime won in the end. It was panto's fault that my first sight of Buckingham Palace was as much of a let down as that frontcloth. Palaces were better in pantomime land, where one also had no problem with Dames being male. Come to think of it, posters at York then were actually in shape and design much more like 18th century playbills and even then one sensed that Theatre had been around for quite a time and would bear investigation.

Hull was a different matter. York in those postwar years had the Minster and cosy tea rooms and enticing, narrow, winding streets. Hull was a ruined wilderness, a bombed out desert of forlorn spaces and rubble. But its New Theatre, breathing in the heady fumes of the nearby brewery, was the home of touring shows, which in the gloomy winter months meant the annual post-London tour of 'Peter Pan'. I don't recall the Hooks, the Wendys, the Peters or even Nana the dog. What I remember is the ship which seemed to rise and fall with the waves and the clock ticking inside the crocodile. How were these things done ? No wonder I became more of a director than an actor.

At home I had my imaginary 'friends, 'Helen' and 'Mrs.Firth', my imaginary world ('Dogton' – well, we had a mongrel dog) , and I remember being much taken by what I now see was the theatricality of the funeral of George the Sixth – three generations of Queens in black veils. But the world of the imagination had to wrestle with practicalities when my Godmother Elsie gave me a Pollock's Toy Theatre (I regret now I never asked her what inspired this choice of present). Much aided by my long suffering mother, rehearsal periods were lengthy and protracted. The cutting out of the characters ('penny plain and twopence coloured'), fitting them into those often recalcitrant wire mounts, learning to handle two characters at once and the script and keep the offstage characters (and their wires !) in some sort of handy order – on the whole easier to cut out those figures on the backs of cereal packets, thread string through the indicated holes and make them dance about.

But my Pollock's Theatre had to have proper programmes and an audience shown to its seats in an orderly fashion. Funnily enough, I preferred the preparation to the performances. Typical director !

Godmother Elsie lived in Worthing and I used to go and stay with her. She was small and doll like and I recall being very worried that she would be blown away as we struggled to the end of Brighton's Palace Pier on a raw and gusty day to see 'Murder at the Vicarage', which I found hard to watch as a rough sea surged and swished very noisily below and I foresaw the imminent collapse of the end of the pier and its show (Late Final : Theatre Drowned; Fatal Loss of small Audience). Back on dry land we went to the repertory theatre in Worthing. I don't remember the play but I see now two 'mannish' ladies with close cropped grey hair and identical black outfits sitting a few rows ahead of us. My queries to my Godmother about this pair were surprisingly easily satisfied by being informed that they were 'regulars – come every Wednesday'. Ah, bliss was it in that dawn to be alive and young and 'innocent' !

At school we were taken to amateur performances by the local branch of the British Empire Shakespeare Society. They are a blank but I remember enjoying the visit to the classroom which would precede them – upright, white haired Colonel Dean with an introductory session. The future director encounters the pre-show talk !

1951 and the Festival of Britain brought the ritual family visit to London. I entered the world of ladies from Surrey doing a matinee after a nice lunch at the Army and Navy, ladies who were asked to remove their hats in a note in the programme you opened by breaking the paper seal with price tag, tinkling selections of Ivor Novello tunes from invisible pit pianos, usherettes in black dresses and white aprons, matinee teas at your seat, curtains (yes, curtains !) rising and falling, entrance rounds, exit rounds, applause for the set (box set, of course), even encounters with the National Anthem (abbreviated). We saw Yvonne Arnaud in 'Traveller's Joy' at the Criterion. My mother recalled Arnaud's membership of the regular cast of the pre-war Aldwych farces as the Underground rumbled down below. Nowadays I pass her neglected memorial in a churchyard on the North Downs above Guildford, where the theatre is named after her. At the Whitehall Theatre we saw 'Reluctant Heroes'; my father remarked that it was the first time he had seen men sitting in the Stalls in their braces and unwittingly we were watching the first of the long post-war run of Whitehall farces. Today the Whitehall Theatre is the two Trafalgar Studios and a farce there would be a surprise.

We didn't go to the cinema much (something to do with 'germs', I suspect) and I was never much concerned about that, though the fare advertised at the Picture Playhouse (the former Corn Exchange) in Beverley's Market Place, noted as we waited in the bus queue, flaunted its allure – 'No Orchids for Miss Blandish', 'Green Grass of Wyoming', The Beautiful Blonde from Bashful Bend', 'Sleeping Car To Trieste'............   But it wasn't 'live', so it didn't really count.

Of course, it couldn't last. The serpent entered the garden. I took an ever greater interest in 'Coming Next' in those programmes I recently gave away as they were taking up so much room – 'White Cargo', 'The Respectable Prostitute', 'LOOK BACK IN ANGER'. Innocence had gone but Theatre had me hooked. And it still has - though now I am as likely to find myself at a site specific or promenade performance as in those West End theatres which suddenly seem cramped, over heated and remarkably short of lavatories. But the boy with his cut out actors on wires , the boy who grew from his toy theatre to work in real theatres, he still directs and happily claims his Senior Citizen concession for another show.

HELEN NICHOLSON

(b. 1958)

Helen's first memories of theatre are vivid, probably because the early 1960s were rather less colourful than might be imagined, though she does remember dancing to The Beatles song 'She loves you' at her first primary school party. She became a teacher in the 1980s, working in schools in Bristol, and leading an Arts Faculty that brought dancers, puppeteers, animation artists and film-makers to young people who regarded participating in the arts as outside their cultural entitlement. In 1992 she became a senior lecturer in Drama Education at Homerton College, University of Cambridge and she is now Professor of Drama and Theatre at Royal Holloway, University of London where she specialises in contemporary practices in theatre education and applied theatre. She is co-editor of *RiDE: The Journal of Applied Theatre and Performance,* and author of *Theatre & Education* (2009), *Theatre, Education and Performance: The Map and the Story* (2011) and *Applied Drama: The Gift of Theatre* (2005), all published by Palgrave.

In her stimulating and important *Theatre and Education* **Professor Nicholson significantly opens with an account of her own first memories of theatre This, of course, is one of several accounts of Pantomime in this book, yet each has its own particular and unique quality:**

My first experience of theatre was a pantomime of *Cinderella* at Golders Green Hippodrome in London in 1962. I was three. I can still picture the comedian Arthur Askey as Buttons, dressed in a dark- blue footman's costume with a matching pill-box hat, telling jokes to a good-humoured audience. I can even remember the jokes,, not so much because I understood them at the time but because they were repeated so often by my father that they became integrated into our family history. To my surprise the programme was recently available on eBay, and my enthusiastic two-quid bid secured me a piece of the history that promised to revive memories of that enchanting matinee. When the programme arrived, my attention was drawn to the eclecticism of the adverts rather than the information about the performance. Corsetiere Mme H. Lieberg presented 'her exclusive collection of international foundation garments', Gilberts Furs Ltd. Offered to repair and remodel fur coats, and, as a part of London University's Extension programme, there were to be '10 Lantern lectures'/ about archaeological exploration. The advertisers were clearly expecting a more affluent audience than my family, and we didn't take advantage of these exclusive offers. Theatre was a rarer and expensive treat, and, sitting on the edge of my tipped-up seat watching a glittering Cinderella go to the ball, I can remember thinking that I was lucky to witness such a magical spectacle.

Helen Nicholson then goes on to share another familiar experience with her readers:

My next memory of theatre is when a group of actors came to perform in my primary school. It must have been about 1964. The school was newly built, having moved from a dark Victorian building where the outside lavatories froze in winter to a bright and airy building with a light hall that had a glass dome in the ceiling. I think the play had something to do with fairy-tale characters, though the details of the plot are hazy. I do vividly remember the thrill of being so close to the characters that I could talk to them, touch their brightly coloured costumes and see the laughter creases in their thick clowns' make-up. What seemed remote, inaccessible and impossibly glamorous at Golders Green suddenly seemed within my grasp. Here were real actors in my school, asking questions and occasionally expecting us to join in the story. My class formed a sizeable audience of forty-eight six-year-olds, and I remember that the teacher, whom we called Mrs Grumpy, took one boy our of the room for ignoring the drama and running around pretending to be a motorbike. I rather regret calling my teacher Mrs. Grumpy. I expect teaching forty-eight six-year-olds every day would test anyone's patience.

Professor Nicholson uses these early experiences to inform and underpin her stimulating idea of the significance of drama in the development of young people but she also evokes some of the optimism that accompanied the provision for drama in the 1960s.

HOWARD LEADER

(b. 1959)

Howard was trained at the Guildford School of Acting and has spent thirty years in the professional theatre touring widely and working rep and in London's West End. His acting highlights include four years with the BBC's *Allo Allo*. Tours include *Piaf, The Snowman, Live Bed Show, Spider's Web, And Then There Were None, Me and My Girl* and *Revenge* among many others and Howard is a regular in pantomime. Howard began broadcasting at Essex Radio in 1984, transferring to the BBC in 1989 when, for five years, he was a presenter on Esther Rantzen's TV show *That's Life!* Since then Howard has continued to combine theatre and broadcasting. His long-running nostalgia music and history programme on BBC Radio Kent transferred to BBC Lincolnshire ten years ago and can be heard every Sunday afternoon between 3 and 6pm on BBC Lincolnshire and BBC Humberside. His work as a reporter and film maker has taken him to Russia, Taiwan, the Ukraine, Bosnia, Malaysia, Croatia, Sierra Leone, Canada, America, Falkland Islands, the Middle East and Afghanistan

Howard entitles these recollections :
Arthur Askey Points the Way

It must have been 1966, when I was seven, that the Cub Scout pack I belonged to advertised a trip to London to see a pantomime. A coach collected us from outside the church in Selsdon and the driver seemed quite unfazed by the thirty or so excited young boys cheering and whooping at the slightest provocation. Our journey ended amid the Christmas lights of Regent Street where we were disgorged outside Liberties and formed a green crocodile which then marched on the London Palladium.

It was the first time I had ever been to a proper theatre and I was at once in awe of the red plush and ornate plasterwork as we entered the foyer. But this, it seemed, was only to collect tickets or directions as we were soon sent through a side door and began climbing an apparently endless staircase which echoed to the burble of the 1st Selsdon Cubs stamping their way up the stone stairs. Finally we reached our goal: wooden doors which opened onto the steep slope of the upper circle. Far below to our right were the great velvet curtains of the stage and to our left the arcs of little red seats seemed to go up and up. Thankfully, there was no more climbing for us as Akala led us straight across to take our seats in the front row of this cliff- side eerie.

The lights dimmed, the band struck up and we cheered, like mad! This was what we had come for, *Robinson Crusoe* had started. I was spell bound. To this day I remember Arthur Askey as the dame singing the *Bee Song.* I remember our being beside ourselves as we yelled at the stupid people on stage who couldn't see that the other was behind them, even though it was completely obvious to all of us. I remember spending a good deal of act two worrying about a native who had staggered on stage with a spear apparently right through his body! Then I spotted him hurling himself about in a dance routine and assumed that spear wounds can't be as serious as I had feared. The whole thing was enchanting, and I was hooked. Henceforth school plays, music and singing would be my main focus, even though my father had a career as an insurance broker in mind for me.

All of this came back to me some twenty three years later when I stepped onto the Palladium stage in the role of General Von Schmelling in the London production of *Allo Allo*. It was our final dress rehearsal and, as we waited for some technical adjustment to lights or sound, Jack Haig (who played LeClerc) remarked "I've waited over seventy years to stand here!" I suddenly felt privileged, I had not waited nearly so long myself, but he had articulated what I had been feeling. Our show ran for over a year and it will always stand of one of my personal career landmarks. A decade later I was back at the Palladium for another eight months in *The Sound of Music* and I would occasionally find myself chuckling at the thought of Arthur Askey standing stage right singing "busy bee busy bee, buzz all yer like but don't sting me!"

I am now a veteran of some 24 professional pantomime productions and each year I tell the story of my first panto experience to some hapless newcomers. Older people have a habit of doing that it seems! But there is a point – that magical evening out with the Cub pack in the mid sixties set the compass for my life. I understood this better many years later, before opening in panto with the great Roy Hudd at Sadler's Wells. In his pre-show pep talk he pointed out that for most children, pantomime is their first experience of the theatre. What they see will shape their view of theatre for years to come, if not for ever. Give them magic, he said, and the magic will stay with them, give them tat and they will not be in our audiences of tomorrow. How right he was, and that is why I passionately believe in the importance of pantomime and the need for all pantomime to be of top quality. Of course, many theatres cannot stage the kind of spectacle I witnessed in 1966, but every player in every performance has to give their all to make their show memorable, day after day, week after week, paying careful attention to the detail of the story telling, the clarity of the gags and the energy of the song and dance numbers. That is the hallmark of a professional production.

Finally, to the other moment which stays in my memory from that night out so long ago. I can sum it up like this. If you were the gentleman sitting in the dress circle below us when, in a particularly exciting moment, I knocked my ice cream tub off the rail above you, please accept my apologies and I hope you like vanilla!

GORDON CLARKSON

(b.1962)

Gordon Clarkson has been a professional entertainer for over 30 years and with his wife Joy runs a small scale production company. He has toured extensively in both their own and other managements' productions and Gordon Clarkson Productions produced the pantomime at the Theatre Royal, Margate (see from cover illustration) for six successful years. He has written the scripts for all their pantomimes and for the half-term children's shows featuring Simple Simon. By contrast, Gordon has also been increasingly involved in taking live entertainment to day centres and residential homes form the elderly. He has appeared in all of his own, original plays.

Gordon accounts for his subsequent passion in a piece entitled *My Theatre-going Childhood* :

People sometimes ask what inspired me to make entertainment my career and, indeed, when we have experienced a particularly fallow period over the years, my wife, Joy, has often posed the same question!
I can only respond by saying that I still have a fondness for and can speak with considerable nostalgia of what is today an almost extinct theatrical medium that led me to make my career in this most interesting, if not always easy, profession. The medium I refer to is best described as 'Light Entertainment' and I was introduced to it by my parents.
Their tastes were not narrow by any means but, although they enjoyed a wide spectrum of music this did not really extend to the 'classics'. The only time that I can recall going to see something mildly 'serious' in my childhood was when my Mum insisted that we visit a London cinema in a heat-wave to see the Royal Ballet's film of 'The Tales of Beatrix Potter'. I am sorry to say that for my brother and me the highlights of this introduction to a classical score were the moments when the quieter passages were drowned by my Dad's snoring. Having never before

experienced the beauty of ballet and classical music we remained, for the time, at least, cocooned in our cultural comfort zone.

So what made up our youthful theatre-going experiences in the 1960s and 70s? We grew up in Thanet and in those days tourism was all important in the towns of Margate, Ramsgate and Broadstairs. It says something of the volume of theatrical choice available in Margate and the, then, posher Cliftonville, that our family rarely ventured to the other towns in search of entertainment.

We were lucky enough to see all of the big stars who came to the Winter Gardens, Margate, for summer seasons and Sunday concerts. In this 1000- seater venue we saw the likes of Tommy Cooper, Frankie Vaughan, Morecombe and Wise, Larry Grayson and the brilliant Danny La Rue along with some of the best supporting acts in the business. We also saw the burgeoning talents of such 'new' stars as Freddie Star and Jim Davidson who would later 'top the bills'. The Winter Gardens actually contained two theatres: the larger auditorium had to stage summer shows 'twice nightly to cater for the enormous demand and, if you bought tickets for the first house (6.15 pm) of the 'big show' you could also then go free of charge to the smaller Queen's Hall to see the aptly –named 'Partytime' summer show which started at 8 pm, provided there were seats available. In this theatre you could enjoy basket meals and drinks at your table and this greatly appealed to my Dad.

In addition to my seeing all of the summer productions and Sunday 'star' concerts at the local authority-run Winter Gardens, my youthful theatrical feast was enhanced by the shows at the nearby Lido complex. This venue boasted live entertainment of some description in all of its bars as well as in a large conventional theatre and in two smaller 'cabaret type' theatres all of which had their own nightly summer season shows! At the Lido theatres, even as a child, I sensed perhaps that things were more 'modest' and looking back now, I think that some of the 'stars' were, in fact, waning! Nevertheless, we saw and enjoyed Tommy Trinder, Charlie Drake and Norman Wisdom leading professional casts in well-produced shows.

But, in the winter, in spite of its 'Winter Gardens' the glamour of professional show business forsook Margate and then we would embark on our magical expeditions to London to see, what I now recognise to have been my true theatrical awakening: the 'Black and White Minstrel Show' Political correctness and a much greater sensitivity to racial issues have rightly made such a show impossible today but it is difficult to describe how every aspect of this event in its various editions was so special to me as a little boy .

For a start, the venue was a glamorous 'West End' theatre. The foyer gleamed with marble and brass, boasting beautifully inlaid doors with bevelled glass. The ornate auditorium featured Stalls, Circle, Upper Circle (the 60s name for the old Gallery) and, unlike any other theatre I had visited, Boxes! The Victoria Palace is a wonderful Frank Matcham design and although I did not fully understand at the time, it appealed to something within me that made me feel that I was 'at home'.

As a family watching the Black and White Minstrels we never sat anywhere other than in the front row on the four seats to the left of the central aisle! By the time we finally got to the Victoria Palace we had usually spent a happy but tiring day in London. My family could not have been aware of just how excited I was at the prospect of seeing the show as we approached the theatre. I would be tingling with anticipation and we would be among the first to go in, promptly half and hour before it was due to start, and make our way to the front stalls. Once we were settled, my Dad would leave us to go to the bar, subsequently leaving it until the very last minute before sprinting down the aisle just before the overture.

I couldn't understand Dad's attraction to the bar when he could have been with us enjoying the sound of the gradual build up of the audience filing into the theatre. This sound still excites me today as I sit in my dressing room hearing the 'house' come over in the tannoy, although, perhaps, this excitement now has more to do with economic reality than anything else!

In due course we began to hear the orchestra tuning up and this marked another milestone on our magical journey to 'curtain up'. Presently, too, we heard the distant bell whose two sharp rings were the cue for my Dad to leave the bar. My tension and excitement rose again, and just as the relief that my Dad had reached his seat in time settled my nerves, so they were tingling again as the dapper Musical Director in his evening tails and white gloves made his way along the inside of the orchestra pit. He was separated from us only by a narrow walkway jutting out from the corners of the stage and running across in front of where, in a few moments' time, the principal singers' feet would be literally close enough for us to touch, if we dared. (We never did!)

The Musical Director would stop on his way to the exact centre of the pit and nod at my brother and me. At the time, I believed that he remembered us from the last time we had seen the show, but now I think it is more likely that he paused in the same place and nodded at the same two seats 14 times a week (the shows were twice nightly) because it was the most convenient place to stop to receive his applause en route for the podium.

Finally the moment had arrived. The house lights dimmed and the M.D's baton pointed down to an unseen corner of the pit cueing a spine-tingling drum role. This accompanied a disembodied but rich voice (I later discovered it was Dai Francis using the off-stage microphone) welcoming us to 'The Black and White Minstrel Show!' Suddenly, and inexplicably seeming to take the audience by surprise, the red velvet curtains flew out to reveal the magnificent minstrels in all their glory. The stage was bright, the costumes and set spectacular and the opening medley was full of harmonious minstrel songs, beginning with 'Ring Ring the Banjo', going into 'Oh Susannah' and 'Polly Wolly Doodle' and others until the last song' There's Going to be a Great Day' finished this sequence 'on a high'.

This was only the first of about a dozen medleys each with a different stage set. These included a moonlit balcony scene with white pillars and turquoise chiffon drapes: the girls wore beautiful pale blue Grecian style gowns and the Minstrel Men silver suits and blue shirts. Today this sounds 'tacky' but then it created a beautiful stage picture that I clearly recall all these years later.

Each medley was like a mini themed production and used to be called a 'scena. They all comprised songs, dances and solos selected to suit the particular vocal style of the principal singers: 'Moonlight and Roses' for the tenor, John Boulter, 'Did you ever get that feeling in the Moonlight' for cheeky Dai Frances or 'By the light of the Silvery Moon' for the honeyed tones of Tony Mercer whose voice, according to my Dad, was reminiscent of someone called Bing Crosby. The ladies were represented by the leggy 'Television Toppers', the charismatic Margaret Savage and a handful of other soloists. One scene change I particularly liked was when a huge piece of sheet music appeared from above the stage and hooked onto the musical notes were the hats, jackets and canes to enable the Minstrel Men to do a costume change without leaving the stage.

So from the moment of that first drum roll right up to the Negro Spirituals Chorus which culminated in 'Michael Row the Boat Ashore' segueing into the big, colourful, show biz finale and 'When the Saints go Marching In' we were treated to a marvellously entertaining live theatre experience. We left the theatre stimulated, entertained and blissfully happy, singing the songs over and over in the train and consigning them to memory until the next time we could forget ourselves in the magic that only live theatre (in whatever form) can provide.

This show, in particular, set that kernel of hope and ambition inside me to have my own career in showbusiness. My dreams of becoming a full-time professional and of touring, writing and producing my own productions and creating a summer show for the Lido, Cliftonville have all been fulfilled. But one thing remains: I am still waiting for an appearance at the Victoria Palace Theatre!

EDITORS' POSTSCRIPT

In compiling and editing this collection of memories and accounts of theatrical activities we have drawn on our own life-long involvement with the theatre and, inevitably, have found resonances with our own experiences. For example, we have devoted some considerable space to the career of John Gielgud . As a young man he would take part in the Shakespeare productions in the Barn Theatre at the home of his aunt, Ellen Terry, Smallhythe Place, Tenterden. This is now owned by the National Trust, and the Barn Theatre is still operating. Anthea was privileged to take *Monday Nights Have Got to be Better,* the play she wrote about the legendary Lilian Baylis, to the Barn in 2008. This play has also been seen twice at Margate's Theatre Royal, a theatre we have mentioned several times in this book because of the important place it holds in the lives of several of our contributors, Similarly, in considering Hugh Walpole's unforgettable description of a first visit to a theatre in his novel *Jeremy,* Anthea was prompted to write:

It reminds me of the first time I took one of my grandchildren to his first pantomime at the age of three. We arrived in time to have a drink in the bar first, but Henry couldn't wait to get into the auditorium. "Can't we go into the theatre *now?*" When we did, his entranced face was a picture: the atmosphere and magic were already working. In the interval he was the first to reach the stage steps, where Gordon Clarkson, playing Simple Simon, was sitting to chat to the children as they purchased their mementos. This was the first of many visits with him to the wonderful Theatre Royal, Margate.

As we glance through the diverse sections of this book, however, the predominance of that peculiarly British phenomenon: the annual Pantomime, becomes obvious. Indeed, of those contemporary practitioners who have contributed, three identified Pantomime as their earliest memory of theatre and three were actually engaged in rehearsals and performance at the time of writing. This family-oriented form of theatrical entertainment is closely followed as a memorable first experience by the children's play *Peter Pan.* Both theatre experiences, of course, depend on fantasy and a rich sense of imagination.

It is, perhaps, inevitable, that so many have mentioned the Pantomime or children's play as key early moments in their imaginative lives because they are art-forms targeted at families and, increasingly, may be the only visit to a live theatre performance to which a young person may be taken. This was almost certainly true in my own case: my first experience of a professional show was a pantomime at a theatre somewhere near Euston Station. My father, who came from a Strict Baptist background sometimes made surprising arrangements as if to challenge his puritan upbringing and I recall sitting in the Circle looking down at the stage. The pantomime must have been *Cinderella* and my most vivid recollection is of one of the ugly sisters (played by a man) appearing wearing only a huge necklace and a pair of enormous bloomers. This particular memory is cemented by recalling my mother's reaction: she 'tut tutted' a lot and thought it 'smutty'.

Anthea, on the other hand, had parents who were obviously more comfortable with the concept of theatre. She recalls:

My parents were always involved in amateur drama so I have been immersed in theatre for as long as I can remember. This had led to a life-long passion for the theatre and theatre-going, although, in my case, I cannot honestly remember the first professional performance I saw.

I do remember that one of the first things in which I participated was the Nativity Play, put on by the Church Primary School I attended and staged in the school hall. As the narrator, I had the onerous task of learning long passages of scripture by heart, whilst everybody else had the fun of dressing up and playing characters. I also remember dancing classes which I attended from an early age and the embarrassment when one year the annual show was staged at the Wood Green Empire: a real theatre! When it came to the turn for my solo I went into the wrong dance because my costumes had been swapped at the last moment and I was left feeling utterly confused.

In my early teens I was cast as Snow White in an amateur production that toured many venues including a prison. The memory of doors closing behind us as we went down long corridors has always stayed with me. Drama also played an important part in the time I spent at Enfield County School, but the headmistress was nevertheless confounded when I announced that I wanted to leave without taking 'A' levels in order to pursue a career in theatre. Whilst attending that school I had spent Saturday mornings outside the Old Vic queuing for gallery seats to see what had become my beloved Shakespeare. I little thought that many years later I would be playing the role of Lilian Baylis, the famous producer at the 'Vic' in my play *Monday Nights have Got to be Better.*

My first professional role was at the Hovenden Theatre Club playing Harriet Skelton in *The Light Within,* a play about the prison reformer Elizabeth Fry who tries to save Harriet from the gallows. Even now I remember the chill of the line 'It takes so long to die with nobody to hang on your legs'. By this time, I had met Harry, whose father had also been immersed in amateur theatre. Marrying young and having five children meant that it was back to amateur drama for a considerable time. When I felt that the children were old enough I took a teaching course at Sittingbourne College, Specializing in drama. This is where I met my current co-editor, Ken, who was a drama lecturer!

After my college years I decided to combine my theatre and teaching experience and undertook work in what would now be termed 'Applied Drama'. I created 'Images Theatre Company' which, for many years took programmes of poetry and Shakespeare to schools and other venues such as Public Libraries. Harry and I found it a great and enduring joy to give so many children what was often their first taste of live theatre. Earlier in this chapter Ken has discussed the important role pantomime has played in people's lives. Significantly, after a performance of *Monday Nights have Got to be Better,* another of the contributors to this book, Gordon Clarkson, offered me a part in his blissfully traditional pantomime. I was delighted to be playing my first fairy in my 60s and have played an assortment of witches and fairies ever since!

Whilst our children were growing up our Christmases were large celebrations involving upwards of 20 people. One year, the children presented a mini Nativity followed somewhat incongruously by a circus complete with prancing horses, a clown and a dancing rabbit. In subsequent years, they and their cousins devised an annual pantomime, and the hours spent devising it, like those children's creations in *Little Women* or the household of Molly Hughes, were richly rewarding, even if the results were sometime hilarious.

In our family, Dickens's *A Christmas Carol* played a central part in the lead-up to Christmas. Harry and I would take turns to read from December the first until the climax on Christmas Eve. As the children grew older, they took their turns at reading and it is gratifying to see one of our daughters continuing the tradition with her young children and that, at any time of year, 'charades' remains a favourite family game. Our children recall being 'dragged along' to rehearsals as well as performances. One of my abiding memories is of Samantha taking her knitting to a rehearsal of *Antigone* 'in case I get bored'. We sat her on a trestle table for a better view and she grew so engrossed in the rehearsal that her knitting took on a very strange shape, full of holes. Sean and Michele both took part in amateur productions for a company to which we belonged and Michelle, Samantha and Gabrielle all went on to become professional dancers. Samantha also stage-managed a professional tour of *Old World* with Images Theatre Company and Sean became a professional photographer, taking wonderful production and publicity photographs for some of our tours.

Whereas Anthea's experiences led to an obvious theatrical slant to the rest of her life and for that of her family, my own path was somewhat different and less direct in its relation to the theatre. However, it did eventually culminate for me in work as a teacher, director, writer and actor and, perhaps above all, in an abiding interest in how we study and discus the phenomenon we call 'theatre'.

 At around the same time as seeing the pantomime I have described I also took part as a soldier and a king in a primary school play and, for this, my mother, who had been a seamstress, forsook her natural suspicion of theatre and made me beautiful costumes that were the envy of my fellow players. However, I suspect that the more significant memory from that period is of a game of charades played at home one Christmas, when my brother, wearing a dressing gown and paper crown portrayed a king in a re-enactment of a nursery rhyme (which we all had to guess). Such home-grown theatricals, of which we have included several examples, sprung from a family which treasured stories and poetry and which provided space and time for creative play and the development of a 'theatre of the mind'. For, by this time, rather like Harold Pinter, I had developed, as so many children do, a company of imaginary characters and friends with whom I could converse at will and whose behaviour could be shaped by my imagination.

By the time I came to take my own children to the theatre pantomimes still 'worked' without the necessity of a 'star' from a TV soap with their often woefully inadequate stage performances. One particular character named Wishy Washy in *Aladdin* entranced them with his ability to lean out over the audience at an angle of 45 degrees from the stage and when the same actor appeared in the following year's pantomime, this feat (obviously achieved by the wearing of boots that hooked into the front of the stage) was eagerly awaited. The song of 'Wishy Washy' became an item in the family's repertoire and theatre –going was established as a part of life that has remained to this day. The results were sometimes unexpected: here, my daughter, recollects her visit to a 'Murder Mystery, highlighting the whole concept of memory and the slender distinction between reality and illusion':

Where to begin? From the raspberry juice or the dark shapes in my bedroom? Or my conversation with Mum and Dad last night? From whatever end, it scarred me for life-or so I like to tease my Mum. On my tenth birthday my Mum (not sure why Dad wasn't involved) arranged a special birthday treat: a tea for friends and then an outing to the theatre. I can't actually remember who was invited but I think it was Helen, Jennifer and Denise. Helen was the one who kept on going on and on about the Bugsy Malone film. Jennifer's dad was a policeman and they lived in the police house near school. Denise went on to be a doctor and we listened to The Sweet together later in a friend's garden shed. But that was a year of so after my tenth birthday.

All I remember about the tea was that mum had made jugs of very pippy homemade raspberry juice. Then with great anticipation we went on to the local theatre to see an Agatha Christie play, controversially named *Ten Little Indians.* Not that I was aware of any controversy at the time. The image that stays with me now from the play is the moment when the lights crash out with a gunshot, silence. Then the lights come up and the judge is sitting on the left of the stage fully robed with this wig on and a rope swings from his hand as he says 'so I took the law into my own hands'. And I realise it was him all along. Even now that phrase makes me shiver….not so much the words but the sing-song mocking tone in his voice-like some weird Stockhausen opera. Mum says she remembers

Helen (who went on to work in the theatre) and I sliding down in our chairs and she thought we were enjoying the horror. All I remember is crying in the car on the way home asking Mum why she had taken us to such a terrifying play. I didn't understand why she was laughing. I think she gradually realised just how spooked I had been when I insisted, for the next year (or so it seems to me now) that I could not go to sleep without the landing light shining through the pane of glass above my bedroom door. The judge with this swinging rope was always possibly there behind the dark outline of the chair in my room

I do not think that my son attended this particular play but I do recall his detailed discussion with me about a production of *Macbeth* in which the cast were dressed in modern military costumes and carried guns. It is tempting to speculate that both my children who now have careers that involve communication skills, imagination, and high levels of literacy and sensitivity acquired at least some of these characteristics through the medium of theatre and performance.

The contemporary pantomime, with its reliance on elaborate technology, so-called 'celebrities' and the pop culture, has abandoned some of the features of that art-form (described earlier by Anthea as 'blissfully traditional') in order to cater for the fact that many children and adults gain their sense of 'reality' from the fiction of television and film. It is a well-known fact that the average British man is more likely to be able to name the characters in a TV soap than to name a number of world leaders. Unfortunately, it becomes all too obvious at a modern pantomime performance that neither children nor adults really know how to behave in a theatre: far from immersing themselves in fantasy, they prefer to yell out replies to comedians on stage, try to understand the 'humour' of jokes that are frequently inappropriate for children or think how remarkable it is that someone from television is there in the flesh. It is even less likely, in these circumstances, that theatre-going will be an established aspect of the lives of the audience because audiences of children often bring so little in terms of creative imagination to the performance.

Throughout this book we have explored the various levels at which theatre can impact on the lives of the young. The most obvious level is the wonderment that is associated with attending a live performance but there is another level in which children make their own theatre. This second level may be organised by a school or similar organisation or within the context of a family. Beyond that is the even deeper level of almost spontaneous theatre which children can create as an aspect of play and that is something which the remarkable teacher and thinker Peter Slade, identified in the immediate post-war years in Birmingham as an essential aspect of maturation. At the deepest level of all there is an 'internal' drama of imagination and fantasy which may, or may not reveal itself in action. This is the level that my six-year- old grandson was exploring when he told us 'When I woke up I couldn't open my eyes and I didn't know if it was real or dreaming: it was horrible!'

The state in which we seem to be neither one thing nor another is now often referred to as 'liminal' by theatre scholars. The 'mechanicals' in *A Midsummer Night's Dream* were toying with this problem when they debated as to how they could get' real' moonlight into the room or how they can convey to the 'ladies' in the audience that the lion is not a 'real' lion but an actor representing one: the same issue provides the magic of a child's first pantomime: 'is this real? Is this imaginary? Why can I talk to the jester from the play in the interval?' And so on. I am convinced that such thoughts need the nurture of home and school and that these environments must be free from limiting prescriptions, constant goals, technology as a substitute for humanity and a lack of conversation.

BIBLIOGRAPHY

Alcott, L.M., *Little Women* (London: Rylee, 1900)

Billington, M., *The Life and Work of Harold Pinter* (London: Faber and Faber, 1996)

Cadogan, M., *Richmal Crompton: the woman behind Just William* (Stroud: Sutton Publishing, 2004)

Crompton, R., *William in Trouble* (London: Newnes, 1927)

Crompton, R., *William the Pirate* (London: Newnes, 1932)

Dickens, C., *Nicholas Nickleby*

Gielgud, J., *Early Stages* (London: Macmillan, 1939)

Grenfell, J., *Joyce Grenfell Request the Pleasure* (London: Macmillan, 1976)

Howland, J., *Memories: a journey through time* (Boughton, Self Published, 1988)

Hughes, M.V., *A London Child of the 1870s* (London: Oxford University Press, 1934)

Nicholson, H., *Theatre and Education* (Basingstoke: Palgrave Macmillan, 2009)

Oliver, E., *Night thoughts of a Country Lady* (London: 1945)

Raverat, G., *Period Piece* London: Faber and Faber, 1934)

Shakespeare, W., *A Midsummer Night's Dream* (Basingstoke: Macmillan Education, 1971)

Sherry, N., *The Life of Graham Greene: Vol. 1.* (London: Jonathan Cape, 1989)

Simmons, D.L., *Margaret Rutherford: a Blithe Spirit* (London: Arthur Barker, 1983)

Wakefield, T., *Forties' Child-an early autobiography* (London: Serpent's Tail, 1980)

Walpole, H., *Jeremy* (London: 1919)

Warren, C.H., *A Boy in Kent* (London: Bles, 1937)

Part of UKUnpublished.co.uk

.CO.UK

UKBookland gives you the opportunity to purchase all of the books published by UKUnpublished.

Do you want to find out a bit more about your favourite UKUnpublished Author?

Find other books they have written?

PLUS – UKBookland offers all the books at Excellent Discounts to the Recommended Retail Price!

You can find UKBookland at www.ukbookland.co.uk

Find out more about **Kenneth Pickering and Anthea Preston** and their books.

Are you an Author?

Do you want to see your book in print?

Please look at the UKUnpublished website:
www.ukunpublished.co.uk

Let the World Share Your Imagination

CPSIA information can be obtained at www.ICGtesting.com
261028BV00008B/185/P